A Place of Grace

FOR MOMS
OF LITTLES

Endorsements

"THIS BOOK IS FOR EVERY mom who's ever prayed, 'Lord, help me parent!' Tackling everything from discipline to anxiety and loneliness, Alexandra's words come alongside you like a friend to encourage, counsel, and whisper a gentle, 'Remember God's grace.' *A Place of Grace for Moms of Littles* is packed with Scripture, wisdom, and thought-provoking questions that will leave every mom feeling confident—not only in her role as a mother, but also in the One she's leaning on—Jesus."

-Erica Renaud

mom of five and author

Pray with Me: Help Your Children Engage in Authentic and Powerful Prayer

"IN *A PLACE OF GRACE for Moms of Littles*, Alexandra Jensen offers women a safe space to feel seen in the joys and struggles of motherhood. Alexandra gracefully ties the truth of God's Word into everyday life, encouraging moms toward sanctification, using Scripture as daily encouragement, and loving the least of these. *A Place of Grace for Moms of Littles* meets you like a smiling friend, encouraging you to grow deeper in your faith and reminding you that you're not alone on the journey of motherhood."

-Whitney Akin

mother of three, speaker, and author

Overlooked: Finding Your Worth When You Feel All Alone

"BEING A MOM THESE DAYS has more challenges than ever. Raising godly kids is tough. Alexandra Jensen shares practical ways to incorporate more Jesus into our lives and our kids' lives in *A Place of Grace for Moms of Littles*. She encourages moms through stories of her own hilarious but real-life mom struggles. Her voice is one of practicality, compassion, and encouragement. I wish there were more books like *A Place of Grace for Moms of Littles* out there for mom followers of Jesus!"

-Lindsay Morris
mom of boys, author
Calling All Princesses

"ALEXANDRA DOES A GREAT JOB presenting not only biblical help but also practical help for moms as well! This book would especially be great for first-time moms trying to figure things out. It is filled with wisdom and insight. The reader will walk away refreshed and with clear direction on how to pursue the Lord in motherhood."

-Katie laPierre
mother of ten, pastor's wife, and author
Eternally Minded Mamas One-Month Devotional and Journal

"A PLACE OF GRACE FOR *Moms of Littles* is a wonderful book. As a slightly seasoned mom with a slew of miniatures across different ages and stages, I find so much worth in the 'Faith Practices' that Alexandra includes in each section to help you find God as you fight the good fight against laundry, sticky handprints, and emotional roller coasters. I also think this book would be a wonderful guiding light to a new mom just setting off on her motherhood path. This is definitely a resource I will share with the mothers I encounter in my ministry. Every mother deserves to know that her work in her home with her children is the most vital personal ministry work she will ever be a part of, and Alexandra does it in the most simple and beautiful way."

-Paige Patterson
mother of four and assistant director of children's ministry
St. Peter's United Methodist Church in Katy, TX

ALEXANDRA JENSEN

A Place of Grace

FOR MOMS OF LITTLES

LIVE SANCTIFIED AND SET-FREE THROUGH CHRIST IN THE MIDST OF CRAZY, BUSY MOM LIFE

AMBASSADOR INTERNATIONAL
GREENVILLE, SOUTH CAROLINA & BELFAST, NORTHERN IRELAND
www.ambassador-international.com

A Place of Grace for Moms of Littles

Live Sanctified and Set-free Through Christ in the Midst of Crazy, Busy Mom Life
©2024 by Alexandra Jensen
All rights reserved

ISBN: 978-1-64960-528-3, hardcover
ISBN: 978-1-64960-693-8, paperback
eISBN: 978-1-64960-569-6

Cover Design by Karen Slayne
Interior Typesetting by Dentelle Design
Edited by Emily Caseres

Ambassador International titles may be purchased in bulk for education, business, fundraising, or sales promotional use. For information, please email sales@emeraldhouse.com.

AMBASSADOR INTERNATIONAL
Emerald House
411 University Ridge, Suite B14
Greenville, SC 29601
United States
www.ambassador-international.com

AMBASSADOR BOOKS
The Mount
2 Woodstock Link
Belfast, BT6 8DD
Northern Ireland, United Kingdom
www.ambassadormedia.co.uk

The colophon is a trademark of Ambassador, a Christian publishing company.

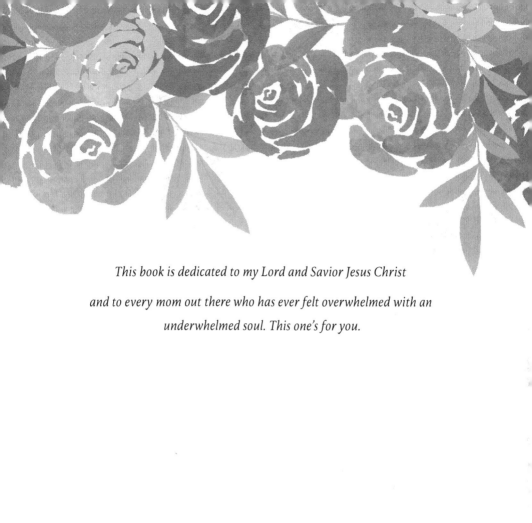

This book is dedicated to my Lord and Savior Jesus Christ

and to every mom out there who has ever felt overwhelmed with an underwhelmed soul. This one's for you.

Table of Contents

AFTERWORD

Introduction

SANCTIFICATION IS A WORK *OF God*. Apart from Christ, we are incapable of living sold-out lives for the Lord. Apart from Jesus, we are immersed in a sea of darkness, lost with no hope of spiritual survival. Apart from Christ, we are incapable of loving others, ourselves, or our children fully. But with God, there is hope. With God, there is light. With God, goodness and mercy freely flow.

Through Christ we are more than conquerors when it comes to loving others and living abundant lives. Because our Redeemer lives, we can do anything and everything the Lord calls us to. In motherhood and in life, we can rise to the occasion of our calling. We can be modern day Esthers and Ruths. We can glean barley from the outskirts of fields with humble hearts. We can raise our voices when God summons us to speak. We can do anything and everything the Lord has called us to.

Motherhood is no cake walk. We must stride out our days, realizing we are in the trenches of everyday mom life, but also knowing and appreciating the fact that these trenches are a mission field. When the Lord called Moses from the burning bush, He said, "'Take off your sandals, for the place where you are standing is holy ground.' Then he said, 'I am the God of your father, the God of Abraham, the God of Isaac and the God of Jacob'" (Exod. 3:5-6). What a grand introduction! I believe that the place where you stand, in your home and in the hearts of your children is holy ground. It is a mission field. The Lord is present, working, and wants to use you on a daily basis.

1

The Lord has called us as moms. We have been chosen as a part of God's divine plan, for His Kingdom purposes in raising up our children in the fear and admonition of the Lord. God wants to use you in some pretty big ways, Mama. It is time for you to rise up and to sanctify your heart, life, mind, and actions to reflect the likeness of Christ.

We are setting an example. We are the biggest role models in our children's eyes. Second to the Lord Himself, you quite possibly could have the most influence and impact in motivating your children's minds and prepping their hearts to receive the Lord. Only the Holy Spirit is capable of changing hearts, but let us not discredit the salience of your role. God wants to do a mountain-moving, mustard-seed-sprouting work in your life and your children's lives. Invite Jesus in. Live sanctified.

A Place of Grace, Not Perfection

I know what you're thinking. Sanctification? I can barely take care of myself and my children, let alone live sanctified. This book is not meant to chastise you. It is meant to highlight the elements of your faith that matter most to you and to God's heart and to propel you further into those things. This is a place of grace, not perfection.

Perfection is like a tropical island—one from which I live far, far away. This book is not about perfection but, rather, how to lead a holy lifestyle, one that is led by the Lord and pleasing to Jesus. I am about to become 100 percent transparent in relating to you as a fallen human being whose only hope is in Christ alone.

I am with you, Mama. I am for you. I am just like you. We wear the same mom-on-the-go sneakers. We are both sporting the same "Mama" cap. I write these words with a baby on my hip. I have multiple mom missions playing ping pong in the back of my mind, as I am sure you do, too. We are in the same boat, Mama!

The truth is I fail at being a mom in so many ways, but God offers me His hope and redemption in full through the resurrection power of the cross. We do not always "got this," but God's got us. And that is what matters, *more than anything.*

Sanctification and the Struggle

1
The Hardest, Best Job

"Be careful not to practice your righteousness in front of others to be seen by them. If you do, you will have no reward from your Father in heaven. So when you give to the needy, do not announce it with trumpets, as the hypocrites do in the synagogues and on the streets, to be honored by others. Truly I tell you, they have received their reward in full. But when you give to the needy, do not let your left hand know what your right hand is doing, so that your giving may be in secret. Then your Father, who sees what is done in secret, will reward you."

Matthew 6:1-4

TO BE A MOTHER IS to be a warrior. We work from sunup to sundown, fighting off the "enemy" in the form of dirty laundry, stinky diapers, hungry little bellies, sleepless nights, sick kiddos, the after-school pickup line, and more—so much more. Motherhood is an extremely tough gig. One of my best friends describes it as "the hardest, best job" she has ever had.

While motherhood is a mountain-climb, let us not neglect the fact that the reward is worth the weight of that mountain in gold; it is priceless. The moment when your little one walks for the first time, when your "baby" graduates from kindergarten, when your child first goes off to an overnight summer camp, when your "little girl" walks down the aisle to say "I do" to the man of her dreams—these are all moments that leave our hearts tied in knots because of the sheer joy and lightning strike of emotions we feel all at once.

These emotions are deeply rooted in the tidal wave of love that we have for our children, harnessed in our hearts. At certain moments in time, there's no stopping the tsunami. There's no impeding its torrential power. Like the force of a freight train, some moments of motherhood leave us breathless, in awe and wonder of the powerful, wonderful God Who created us in His very own likeness, the One we serve and call, "Abba, Father."

These moments of realizing the full force of the love we have for our children are deeply rooted in God's love for us in being His image bearers. God loves us infinitely, more than we could ever imagine. We love our children in a similar way that God loves us because we reflect His image. As the Creation story reminds us, "So God created mankind in his own image, in the image of God he created them; male and female he created them" (Gen. 1:27).

On the other end of the spectrum of motherhood, there are days that feel excessively difficult and demand an extra helping of our tender love and care. When our kids are sick, dad is out of town, a busy season at work requires more of our time and energy, the days are cold and rainy and the kids seem to be on catnip but cannot go outside to let out their inner wild things—these days make being the best mothers that we can be all the more challenging.

We must dig in our heels and pull the rope with all our might. We are in a tug-of-war battle for our children's hearts. The role we play in leading our children to Jesus is instrumental, and our influence in their faith walk is monumental.

You may not get a purple heart in the process, but know that God's heart notices every ounce of effort you pour into your children. He sees you going above and beyond, giving this thing called life and motherhood your all! God notices, even when no one else does. He will reward you one beautiful day. Rest on this truth, have grace for yourself, and realize that all you do has eternal value and is beautiful in Jesus' sight. Walk assured knowing that the God of this universe sees you and cares. You are infinitely loved.

Humbling Moments

Sometimes, I like to think I'm great at this mom thing. It was Halloween, and I was eight months pregnant. We had been invited over to a friend's house to go trick-or-treating. I had all the kids costumed and ready. My daughter, Emma Claire, was a well-known cartoon train character and absolutely in love with her outfit. She adores this particular train, and for her to become him was like living in some fairytale fantasy. My almost two-year-old son, Josiah, was the cutest little blond mouse you have ever seen. I even had a pumpkin suit on myself. Their pumpkin buckets were in the car, and the brownies I was bringing were neatly organized on a jack-o'-lantern plate. After buckling my two toddlers into their car seats, we were on our way. I felt like supermom.

We had made it about two miles down the road when I began to hear whimpering, which became muffled crying, and finally gagging. Then it happened. "Blahhhh!" Sweet, little Emma Claire had thrown up all over herself.

The nausea medicine! I forgot the nausea medicine! I realized immediately. Emma gets carsick easily; and anytime we are going to be driving for more than five minutes, I have to give her half of a kid's chewable nausea tablet.

Immediately, I whipped the car around and drove home, still determined to attend our trick-or-treating plans. I got Emma out of the car and tried to scoop some of the vomit out of her car seat and wipe it down, knowing that the car seat would never be the same. Emma was still crying as I let Josiah out of his car seat and put him in the house. I tried to wipe her down and clean her up as best as I could. I rummaged around and found her last year's costume, which still barely fit. I put a big red bow in her hair, and we were all set.

"Josiah!" I called, ready to put him back in his car seat. "Josiah! Josiah? Josiah!" I shouted.

I could not find Josiah and went into an immediate state of shock and panic. My fight-or-flight response kicked in, and I began running around the front of our house yelling his name, desperate at this point. Surely, he had not dawdled down the street. I almost began to cry when I heard giggling coming from somewhere inside the house. My almost-two-year-old was standing behind the door of the study hiding and laughing at Mommy having a panic attack.

"Josiah Jensen!" was about all I could say as I scooped him up and buckled him into his car seat. With my two cute mice now in tow, we were finally on our way.

Humbling moments like these in motherhood remind me that God is in control. He is in control of our hearts. He is in control of our lives. He is in control of our children. God is in control, and I am not. Moments like these force me to remember that God is the true Parent, and I am only a vessel. The Lord deserves all of the glory, honor, and recognition in this wild and crazy thing called motherhood and life.

Paul the Apostle was in a jail cell when he wrote these world-renowned words: "I know what it is to be in need, and I know what it is to have plenty. I have learned the secret of being content in any and every situation, whether well fed or hungry, whether living in plenty or in want. I can do all this through him who gives me strength" (Phil. 4:12-13). Paul experienced challenges different from the ones we face as moms, but we, too, can do all things through Christ when we rely on the Lord as our daily strength. We too can learn, "the secret of living in every situation." By trusting in God to make a way, by relying on the Lord as our daily strength, and by depending on His life-changing presence, our hearts can thrive through all things.

When we trust in God as our portion, the Lord enables us to do so much more than we ever thought possible. When we open our arms and hearts to Jesus, the diameter of all that we can hold is divinely widened as Christ carries our burdens and replaces our worries with the yoke of His peace. Jesus spoke to His disciples' doubt with these comforting words: "'With man this is impossible, but with God all things are possible'" (Matt. 19:26).

While we love loving on our babies, handing out popsicles, and hearing our children laugh and play, there are many other components of motherhood that are far less desirable. These ordinary, sometimes sticky tasks strengthen our faith and develop our servant hearts to reflect and model the love of Jesus Christ. While our hard work goes seemingly unnoticed at times, we are acutely noticed by our Heavenly Father, all the time.

Dear Jesus,

Thank You for noticing me. When it feels like the world does not realize or care, I lean into You and Your Word, trusting that You do recognize me and deeply care. You care about the hard work and effort I pour out as a mom; but even more so, You care about the conditions of my heart.

Along the way, I pray that You would cultivate a mindset of thanksgiving within me. Create in me a grateful heart. Instill in me a longing to do Your holy work by serving my family faithfully because of my faith in You. I am wholly Yours, Jesus. Do a beautiful ridding of self-work in me. Infuse me with strength, diligence, and joy in doing Your sacred work today. Thank you for the gift of motherhood.

In Jesus' mighty Name I pray, amen.

Steps of Faith:

A step of faith is an application checkpoint. How can you live out the chapter's message and take a step of faith toward the cross? Some days will seem like baby steps while others feel like giant leaps! Let us live out our calling as mothers in Christ and walk by faith.

- Meditate on these words from 2 Corinthians: "For we live by faith, not by sight. We are confident, I say, and would prefer to be away from the body and at home with the Lord. So we make it our goal to please him, whether we are at home in the body or away from it" (2 Cor. 5:7-9).

- Acknowledge God today as you go about doing your daily tasks. Dwell on Philippians 4:13. I love how the Amplified Version of the Bible explains it: "I can do all things [which He has called me to do] through Him who strengthens *and* empowers me [to fulfill His purpose—I am self-sufficient in Christ's sufficiency; I am ready for anything and equal to anything through Him who infuses me with inner strength and confident peace]" (Phil. 4:13).

- Talk to Jesus out loud while driving in your car, folding the laundry, preparing meals, getting dressed and ready for the day, or praying in your closet on your hands and knees. Pray!

2
Bible-Check!

"For the word of God is alive and active. Sharper than any double-edged sword,
it penetrates even to dividing soul and spirit, joints and marrow; it judges the
thoughts and attitudes of the heart."

Hebrews 4:12

NO BIBLE COULD BE FOUND on my desk. Planner—check! Notepad—check! Christian self-help book—check! Computer—check! Empty baby bottle—check! Fun pens! Check, check! Bible—nope. I realized right then and there that I needed to make God's Word a priority in my life.

Since that day of discovering no Bible on my desk, I have placed reading God's Word first on the forefront of my heart and life. More than my morning coffee, makeup on my face, social media, or the news, I need God's Word running through my veins. Although this does not always look like waking up before sunrise to crack open my Bible, reading God's Word has become a daily cornerstone in my life.

Whether it is during naptime, in the morning, while your kids are at soccer practice, or after your kids go to bed, read God's Word. It will rearrange your heart and direct your daily life. Through reading the Bible, we invite Jesus to become our best Friend, reigning over our minds, ruling our hearts, overflowing into our words, and molding us into ambassadors of the Lord Most High. Christ gives us His peace and equips us to bless

12

others through His Word (2 Pet. 1:3). All of our hearts' desires can be found in one holy book.

Fair warning: the heart alterations the Bible sews up inside of you may not always be convenient or comfortable. The Holy Spirit has a way of piercing our very souls with the needle and thread of God's truth. The truth will put a spotlight on the sin in your life. The truth will remind you to go the extra mile in loving others and living for Jesus. "'The truth will set you free'" (John 8:32).

The Word can bring the darkness of hidden sin in our lives into the light. Praise Jesus that darkness and light cannot coexist! Through God's Word, Jesus can throw back the covers of our lives and awaken us to the sin slumbering in the beds of our hearts that would have otherwise remained sleeping and unnoticed. Praise God for His faithfulness in revealing to us our sins and offering His forgiveness in full to those with repentant, sincere hearts.

Jesus' presence shows up when we read God's Word. The Holy Spirit will come in and tug on your heart throughout the day when you read the Bible and pray. *Help your neighbor. Assist that friend in need. Befriend that lonely mother.*

The Holy Spirit will call you out and command you to obey. Listen for the Holy Spirit's promptings throughout the day. Jesus' voice becomes much more audible when we are reading the breathing, active, life-giving, heart-changing, emotion-evoking, truth-revealing, fruit-producing Word of God. Christ's silent but sure voice echoes loudly throughout the pages of Scripture.

One way to study God's Word is through journaling. Below is a list of questions that I use during my Bible study journaling time. After reading a portion of Scripture, answer the following questions:

1. What is the main point of the passage?
2. What does this teach you about the nature of God?

3. Does this verse connect with or remind you of any other verses? Write them out.

4. How can you apply this knowledge of Scripture to your life? Ask yourself, "How can I live this truth?"

If you have time to write out a prayer, I highly encourage you to do this as well! Writing out prayers is powerful and effective. Even if your prayers seem repetitive for a period of time, write them out. We can tangibly see evidence of God's faithfulness through the fruit of answered prayers when we journal our thoughts to God.

Have grace for yourself. There are going to be some days that we really and truly do not have time to read the Bible and journal our thoughts to God. But be diligent; be persistent. If you don't have time to do all of the above, I challenge you to do some of it. The best way to receive the fullness of God's life-giving grace is through His powerful, holy Word.

As Jesus prepared His disciples for His leaving this world after His death on the cross, Thomas was not convinced they would know the way to go afterward, asking, "'Lord, we don't know where you are going, so how can we know the way?' Jesus answered, 'I am the way and the truth and the life. No one comes to the Father except through me'" (John 14:5-6).

God's Word shows us the way. Like a flashlight, or a candle in the dark, the Bible illuminates our lives *when we read it*! It compels us to forgive. It calls us to love others. It commands us to tell the truth. It demands we live boldly for Christ and speak the name of Jesus. God's Word sanctifies our hearts and reorders our lives.

Dear Jesus,

Thank You for the Word. Thank You that You are the Word (John 1:1, John 14:6)! Thank You for the promises You provide, the hope You assure, and for the joy You bring to my heart. Thank You, Jesus, for loving me and enabling me to meet with You through the Divine provision of Your holy Word.

In Jesus' wonderful Name, amen.

Steps of Faith:

- Get into God's Word today! If you don't know where to begin, start in the book of Romans. It is a chapter of the Bible written by the apostle Paul that beautifully illustrates the Gospel.
- Start a Bible study. A few that I would highly recommend are *Seeing Jesus in the Old Testament, 40 Days Through the Bible,* or any study by Beth Moore or Lysa TerKeurst.
- Review the following verses and reflect on the fact that Jesus is the Word of God. When we read the Bible, we are ultimately communing with Christ.
    - "In the beginning was the Word, and the Word was with God, and the Word was God. He was with God in the beginning. Through him all things were made; without him nothing was made that has been made" (John 1:1-3).
    - "Jesus answered, 'I am the way and the truth and the life. No one comes to the Father except through me'" (John 14:6).

3
Salty Lives

"Fix these words of mine in your hearts and minds; tie them as symbols on your hands and bind them on your foreheads. Teach them to your children, talking about them when you sit at home and when you walk along the road, when you lie down and when you get up."

Deuteronomy 11:18-19

DISCIPLING SMALL CHILDREN CAN BE challenging because their attention span is that of a butterfly. However, a few things that have helped me immerse my children in the knowledge and love of Jesus are reading Bible stories with them each day, listening to praise and worship music in the car, praying with them before they go to bed and before meals, and giving them the opportunity to pray. These are simple endeavors—nothing exceptionally unique or new—but the key is consistency.

Little ones need structure and repetition in their lives. This includes studying God's Word and weaving its principles into their daily lives. Read God's Word to your children and pray, each day. It all trickles from the top! We must be in our Bibles, seeking the Lord for ourselves, striving to grow "in wisdom and stature, and in favor with God and man" (Luke 2:52). God's Word in our lives comes alive and spills out of our hearts when we are seeking Jesus fervently, adamantly, and consistently.

Every morning, we take off like racehorses out of the chute as moms, striving to meet the demands of our families. In all of our striving, may we choose to remember that by His stripes we have been healed. Let us not forget to make time for Jesus. Whether it is early in the morning, late in the afternoon, in the evening, or at midnight, we need Jesus and God's Word alive in our lives, governing our hearts, minds, and hands.

Approach getting to know the Lord through reading and studying the Bible the way you would get to know a friend. Go inside the restaurant. Sit down and enjoy God's Word. Don't treat the Bible like it's a fast-food drive-through.

Getting into God's Word for yourself might be the very best way to teach your children the beauty and value of having a relationship with Jesus. What greater gift could you offer your family than being a God-fearing woman, a mother whose heart, mind, soul, and strength beats solely for Jesus? This is "the first and greatest commandment," according to Jesus—the gold standard we are called to as Christ followers (Matt. 22:36-37).

Always Watching

Our children are taking notes, no doubt. I want my children's notes to have crosses, Bibles, and scribbles of Jesus holding Mommy's hand all over them. I want my kids to know that I love God and that God loves them even more than I do! I want my little ones to establish a love for the Lord at an early age. I want them to grow up to be spiritual leaders, men and women who love Jesus and lead others to the cross. I want them to shine God's light. I want them to live salt-filled lives, loving others and walking the extra mile with Jesus daily because of the love, joy, peace, and ultimate satisfaction they find in His presence.

I wish all of these things for my children, as I am sure you do, too. Therefore, we must cultivate godly attributes within our own hearts and adopt daily disciplines in our lives that are centered around Christ. He is the Rock, the firm Foundation of our lives.

In order for our children to have a model to go by, we must seek the Lord and exude His brilliance. Our treasure must be found in Christ alone. Invest your time, talent, and treasure in His Kingdom purposes. Use your spiritual gifts to glorify the Creator (1 Pet. 4:7-11).

The only perfect model of a heart fully on fire for God is Christ Himself, but we are called to shine brightly for Jesus and transpose the warmth of His love. In this dark world, we are called to bring the campfire glow, to live salty lives of love for our children and the world to see. Listen to what Jesus told His followers about their influence for the Kingdom:

> "You are the salt of the earth. But if the salt loses its saltiness, how can it be made salty again? It is no longer good for anything, except to be thrown out and trampled underfoot. You are the light of the world. A town built on a hill cannot be hidden. Neither do people light a lamp and put it under a bowl. Instead they put it on its stand, and it gives light to everyone in the house. In the same way, let your light shine before others, that they may see your good deeds and glorify your Father in heaven" (Matt. 5:13-16).

In order to mold our children's little hearts and minds to know Jesus, we must know Him for ourselves. We must seek Jesus each day. We must be in our Bibles and pray. We must actively pursue the Lord in our daily lives. This sets an example for our children and provides an arrow pointing them in the direction of what matters most—Christ's Kingdom.

Children's minds are astonishingly malleable. We must realize this fact and strive to mold them according to the knowledge and love of the Gospel of Christ at an early age. Jesus will help us along the way. We are not called to change our children's hearts; only the Holy Spirit is capable of this awesome wonder. We are called to teach our children God's Word and be living examples of Christ's love.

Dear Heavenly Father,

I pray that my children come to know You and love You someday. Help me be faithful in discipling my children. Show me ways that I can be an arrow pointing upward to You and Your Kingdom expansion plans.

In Jesus' holy Name, amen.

Steps of Faith:

- Immerse your children's minds in wholesome music. Purchase a CD or download kid-friendly worship music that you can listen to with your children in the car.
- Strive to incorporate Jesus into the conversations you have with your children today.

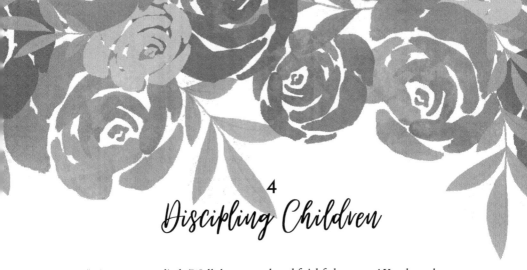

4
Discipling Children

"His master replied, 'Well done, good and faithful servant! You have been faithful with a few things; I will put you in charge of many things. Come and share your master's happiness!'"

Matthew 25:21

I HAVE THREE CHILDREN: EMMA Claire, Josiah, and Baby Madison. They are precious not only to me but also to the Lord. God has entrusted me with this valuable "gold." In light of this parable, it is my job to teach my children the Good News of Jesus Christ. When my time comes, on that blessed day, I want the Lord God to be able to look at me and confidently say, "Well done, good and faithful servant!"

God cares about your faithfulness as a mom. It is your God-given assignment to let the light of Christ shine brightly in your life for your children to see. Through its warmth and loving glow, may your children come to know Jesus and be attracted to the lantern of God's love illuminated in your life. May they take up and carry the torch of Jesus for themselves. Disciple your children faithfully and let God take care of the results.

Regardless of what your children choose to do someday with the seeds you have sown, we have been called to teach our children about Jesus through God's Word. While we hope and pray that someday our children will receive Christ and cultivate a thriving relationship with the Lord for themselves, we are called to be faithful sowers when they are young. We can continue to help our children thrive in their relationships with Christ as they enter adulthood, but it is imperative we impart godly wisdom and teach faith-filled lessons to our children when they are small. Don't wait! It's never too early to teach your children about Jesus.

Gymnastics

I remember being a little girl and doing gymnastics for the first time. I was fearless. I would do anything and everything the coaches prompted me to do. Round off, check! Back handspring, you've got it! I was a daredevil and able to be well-trained. As I got older, by the time I was about nine years old, my fear of executing new tricks kicked in. I became hesitant and would let my mind slip into worst case scenario pitfalls.

Those early years of gymnastics were foundational to help me establish basic skills. My fear and own mental judgment did not get in the way when I was really little; but as I got older, the switch gradually began to flip. I was still a great gymnast. But those fears that would come into play did hold me back a degree from being the best gymnast I could possibly be. I went on to do cheerleading in high school and college. There are no regrets. But if I were to do it all over again, I would have trained harder when I was younger.

I remember one important tip one of my gymnastics coaches taught me that helped me to face my fears in doing a standing back tuck unassisted. It was so simple, yet mind-altering. He said to me, "Trust the form." He did not say "trust yourself." He told me, "Trust the form," implying that having the correct form would enable me to execute the skill safely. The first time I did a standing back tuck by myself, I landed on my knees, but I did not break my neck! With practice, I was able to perfect the skill by trusting the correct form. Eventually, I developed a muscle memory that enabled me to do a standing back tuck with ease.

I cannot help but think about how this applies to our faith. When we trust in the Lord in the strength of His might (Eph. 6:10) and depend not on ourselves but on His Word and will, we are able to live life with the safety and security of knowing that Jesus is by our side.

God's way is the best way. We learn the "correct form" through His Word. Eventually, we must trust in that form and walk by faith, executing all that God has called us to as mothers and Christ-followers.

We must live boldly for Jesus. Although we might be afraid at times, if we trust in the form of Jesus through God's Word, we will be safe. We can be confident in carrying out the Lord's will in knowing God is spotting us with His righteous right hand. Jesus will always aid us through what He has called us to.

Paul's letter to Timothy calls us to focus our time and energies on training for godliness, saying, "Have nothing to do with godless myths and old wives' tales; rather, train yourself to be godly" (1 Tim. 4:7). The word "gymnastics" comes from the Greek word *gumnazo*, which means to exercise or to train. We must become gymnasts in a godly sense, training our hearts and hands to exercise the Lord's will. We must execute leaps of faith and mentally rely on our trust in Jesus. We must depend on God's Word to understand the "correct form" and develop the muscle memory of godliness by practicing it in our daily lives.

We must impart godly wisdom to our children when they are young. Before doubt and the ways of the world creep into their minds, we must help our children develop into the best gymnasts for Jesus that they can be.

In discipling children when they are little, we have the advantage of molding their hearts and minds to be attuned to the Spirit of the Living God. They can develop the muscle memory of godliness and adopt a love for Jesus for themselves with proper training. Teach your children to "trust the form" of God's Word in their hearts and lives.

The book of Jeremiah describes the natural condition of our hearts, saying, "The heart is deceitful above all things and beyond cure. Who can understand it?" (Jer. 17:9). Now, more than ever, we must teach our children to rely on God's Word. Over what their teachers might say, over their feelings and desires, we must teach our children to trust in God's Word to know how to live their lives.

We live in a confusing day and age for children. This is no secret. The culture of our world is immersed in sin. We must depend upon God's Word like never before, teaching our children to fully rely on the Lord and what the Bible says. Jeremiah 17:9 is such a good heart checkup for us to keep on the forefront of our minds. When faced with overriding feelings, emotions, and heart desires, we must trust in God's Word above all else, weighing our choices and focus against what the Lord has to say.

"The fear of the Lord" is caring about God's opinion more than the opinions of others. Living in the fear of the Lord means that we focus on what matters most to the heart of God before chasing after our own inclinations and desires. Follow God's Word, not your heart. The heart is wicked, and feelings can be contrary to the Lord's opinion. Before you listen to your heart, listen to the Holy Spirit and follow the ways of God's Word.

God has good plans for you and me. Trust in that. God's best and the Bible will never contradict or cancel each other out. Satan would like nothing more than to trick us into taking matters into our own hands, coursing our lives based on the feelings of our hearts. Do not accept or cave into this lie. The upstanding Word of God is the only thing we can depend upon as solid-rock Truth in our lives. God's Word never fails (Luke 1:37).

Roots

There is a plant growing in our backyard that is an invasive species. It is a ground-covering weed commonly known as "Fig Buttercup." The weed takes root and threatens to spread across the entirety of a yard or field if not exterminated.

Surprisingly, children's hearts work much the same way but positively. When we begin to teach them godly principles through correction and explicit teaching from the Bible, the root of godly standards penetrates their lives. Their love for God grows and grows as they are led and fed the Word of God and have the light of our example to go by. So long as we are encouraging our children's spiritual growth, they will likely have such a widespread love of the Lord that any weedkiller the world tries to spray their way would be unable to reach and cover all of the roots that have already taken place.

Do the groundwork. Disciple your children through godly discipline. Adopt daily habits that include reading the Word of God and praying with your children. Minister to your children's hearts when opportunities arise by speaking the name of Jesus and giving God glory. Live a life of worship for your children to see. We need to be rooted in Jesus Christ, our lives centered around him so that our children's baby roots begin to thrive and dig deeper into God's love as they search for the Living Water deep in their hearts.

Listen to the words of Paul spoken to the baby church of Ephesus: "'Now I commit you to God and to the word of his grace, which can build you up and give you an inheritance among all those who are sanctified'" (Acts 20:32). Paul was about to leave and continue on his missionary journey. He left the Ephesians with this final message after teaching them everything he knew. Then, he let go. Eventually we will have to do the same.

Our children will grow up and move out of our homes someday. While they are young, we can impress the Bible into their hearts and speak the name of Jesus over their lives. But eventually, they will have to make a decision for themselves. We can let go gradually by giving our children opportunities to choose Christ for themselves through church camps, Vacation Bible School, youth group, Christian summer camp, mission trips, and so much more.

Give your children ample opportunities to choose Christ for themselves at an early age. Follow the admonition of Jesus: "'Do not hinder them, for the kingdom of heaven belongs to such as these'" (Matt. 19:14).

> *Dear Jesus,*
> *Thank You for today! Thank You for the opportunity I have to immerse my children in the knowledge of Your love and grace. Thank You for Your life-giving truth found in God's Word. Please help me to be diligent in teaching my children about You through the Bible. Give me grace and discipline in*

this endeavor. In teaching my children about You, I pray that Your Holy Spirit will meet me halfway and do all of the heavy-lifting. Thank You for Your peace and presence in my life.

In Jesus' everlasting Name I pray, amen.

Steps of Faith:

- Some fantastic resources that have been gems in helping me disciple my children include the following:
  - www.life.church/media/early-childhood (Bible story videos)
  - www.kidscorner.net/bible-stories (Audio Bible stories)
  - *The Jesus Storybook Bible* by Sally Lloyd-Jones (A children's Bible that tells God's Word through beautifully written stories and illustrations)
  - God Talks With Kids Faith-Building Conversation Starters (facebook.com/GodTalksWithKids)
  - *365 Read Aloud Bedtime Bible Stories* by Daniel Partner (A read-aloud Bible storybook)
  - *Pray With Me: Help Your Children Engage in Authentic and Powerful Prayer* by Erica Renaud. (This book is meant for parents. It teaches practical ways to pray with your children, and how to encourage them to adopt the practice of faith-packed prayer for themselves.)
- In some way, shape, or form, read the Bible to your children today. Using a children's Bible or your own, a Psalm or an Old Testament Bible story, read God's Word.

5
Surrendering Control

"Many are the plans in a person's heart, but it is the Lord's purpose that prevails."

Proverbs 19:21

I LIKE TO BE IN control. I would not define myself as a "control freak," but I like to have control over my life (and sometimes my children's). Guilty as charged—yes, I know. Can you relate?

The truth is many of us like having a sense of control over our children. As a parent, this is a tough battle. Some control is okay, and boundaries are necessary. Healthy parameters help our children feel safe, secure, and confident. But we also have to know when to let go and allow the Holy Spirit to do His sacred work inside of our children's hearts and lives.

Until we surrender our control and become subordinate under God's control, whether it be in our lives or the lives of our children, we are simply fish swimming in circles, hamsters spinning on wheels. We may think we are making strides of success when we see our children behaving and shining in terms of outward appearances; but if we have not included Christ in the conversation when it comes to discipline, we have merely created little toy robots who act out of fear instead of their love for God. Our discipline must be heartfelt, intended to reset our children's minds to focus on and please Jesus.

The other day I was in a children's resale shop, acquiring summer clothes for my kids, when I noticed a mom reprimanding her child. She had the most hateful voice as she threatened her child with what sounded like it would be an almost violent spanking. It was horrific to overhear. "I am going to make you dance, whipping your butt." The child shot me a look that said she knew she had been wronged.

Children know when we lose our tempers and are disciplining out of anger, impatience, and impulse instead of love. I wanted to tap that mama on the shoulder and tell her, "There's a better way. His name is Grace. His name is Love. His name is Jesus." But in the heat of the moment, I knew that was not what she or the child needed. So I said a silent prayer, instead: *Dear Jesus, help this mama to discipline her child with a spirit of love and not hate. Help her to redirect her child in a way that is spiritually meaningful and pleasing to you, Lord. Give her discernment, patience, and self-control. Show her there's a better way, God. Teach her Your ways of loving, Christ-focused discipline. Cultivate an awareness of the conditions of her own heart and a desire to want to please You in all areas of motherhood. Help me with these things as well. In Jesus' holy Name, amen.*

Discipleship and discipline go hand in hand. You cannot be successful at one of these things without the other. Part of your role as a Christian parent is to discipline your child in a godly manner, according to God's Word.

Discipline is a way that we can get our children to behave, to fall in line and become respectful and obedient under our authority. However, if their hearts are not changed in the process, then our means of discipline and control are utterly useless. It is like how Jesus described the Pharisees—a clean cup on the outside with a filthy interior (Matt. 23:25). Empty discipline that is harsh and ineffective in steering our children closer to Jesus is detestable to the Lord. Jesus instructs us to, "'First clean the inside of the cup and dish, and then the outside also will be clean'" (Matt. 23:26).

A child's heart that loves the Lord desires to do what is right. Our kids will continue to mess up and sin, but we can be hopeful that they will learn from their mistakes and turn to Jesus when we direct them through heartfelt discipline to the Bible and God's love. What does heartfelt discipline look like? Heartfelt discipline is delivered calmly, through rational thinking, help from the Holy Spirit, and God's Word.

If my toddlers were taking toys away from each other, I might ask, "Emma, how do you think it made Josiah feel when you took away his toy?"

"Sad," she would probably say.

"Emma, sweetie, do you want to make your brother feel sad? We need to be kind and loving. That is what Jesus would want. What could you have done instead?"

Maybe she would respond, "I could have asked Josiah if I could play with the toy or wait my turn."

But it is likely my three-year-old might not come up with this well-rehearsed answer yet. (We are working on it!) I would probably need to feed her the answer and ask her to practice this alternative.

Keep it simple and to the point. Ask them lots of thought-provoking questions. Incorporate the language of emotions: sad, mad, glad, upset, disappointed, excited, energized, tired, unfair, exhausted, overlooked, overwhelmed. Help them to explore and realize these things through verbalization. Our goal is not to quench their feelings but to teach them how to recognize and regulate their emotions in a manner that is acceptable, expressive, and God-honoring.

Insert Jesus' name. Remind them that God's unfailing love and faithfulness catches us, even when we fall off the tightrope in our lives. Teach them the meaning of God's grace through a demonstration. Use "we" language instead of "you" language to let them know that you are on their team. It does not have to be constant, but try using the word "we" instead of "you" from time to time. This lets your child know you are for them.

Walk them through the correct behavior and have them verbally and physically rehearse the desired outcome. Practice makes perfect. Although our children will never be perfect, they can reap the harvest and benefits of a heart that is overflowing with goodness and Christ's love. We must make this our goal in discipline.

Do not tie them to their sin. Instead, identify their offense as an action separate from their identity. Your children are not "mean," "rude," or "disrespectful." Their offense may have been, but be sure to remind them of who they are as beautiful from the inside out, compassionate, Christ-honoring creations of the Lord God.

Paul gives us a powerful picture of what relationships in Christ should look like:

> In your relationships with one another, have the same mindset as Christ Jesus: Who, being in very nature God, did not consider equality with God something to be used to his own advantage; rather, he made himself nothing by taking the very nature of a servant, being made in human likeness. And being found in appearance as a man, he humbled himself by becoming obedient to death—even death on a cross! (Phil. 2:5-8).

In our relationships with our children, we are not to use our positions of power to pump up our egos. Like Christ, we are to humble ourselves in reverence of the Lord and raise up our children with the love of Jesus cascading out of our hearts. We are to be diligent in disciplining our children but with the goal of drawing out our children's hearts for Jesus in the process.

Keep God's Word on the forefront of your mind when disciplining. The goal of discipline is to point our children to the Bible, and the heart of God. Reference the Fruits of the Spirit. Use words and phrases like, "kind," "loving," "patient," "generous," "giving," "caring," and "thoughtful of others."

Do your best to verbally incorporate Scripture:

- "Love your neighbor as yourself" (Mark 12:31).
- "Blessed are the peacemakers" (Matt. 5:9).
- "Children, obey your parents" (Eph. 6:1).
- "A gentle answer turns away wrath" (Prov. 15:1).
- "Gracious words are a honeycomb" (Prov. 16:24).

Think of the attributes of love, as described in the Bible, as the lesson you are trying to teach: "Love is patient, love is kind. It does not envy, it does not boast, it is not proud. It does not dishonor others, it is not self-seeking, it is not easily angered, it keeps no record of wrongs. Love does not delight in evil but rejoices with the truth. It always protects, always trusts, always hopes, always perseveres" (1 Cor. 13:4-7).

We can check our own hearts in the mirror with these verses as well! It takes a patient, God-fearing parent to administer discipline in a godly manner. We must be actively seeking the Lord through His Word. In order for the Word to overflow and spill out of us when a child's disobedience strikes, we need to be filled to the brim with the words and truths that can be found only in our Bibles. Instead of anger, rage, and malice, we want the Word of God to well up inside of us when our children disobey. God's Word alone has the power to direct us in delivering consequences, with a Bible-based admonition, that will cause our children's hearts to scoot a little bit closer to Jesus.

I am not an expert on discipline, but I know a Man Who was. His name is Jesus. In correcting people and bringing their sin to light, Jesus asked a lot of thought-provoking questions. He made people realize for themselves that they had indeed sinned against God. That is the goal of heartfelt discipline. We want our children's hearts to be changed and for them to see their sin for themselves and want to do better for Jesus. We want our children to take charge of their own behavior and to strive for diligence and the fruits of the Spirit in their daily lives because that's what Jesus would do. We want our children to please us; but first and foremost, we want the conditions of their hearts, attitudes, and minds to please the Lord.

Who Is in the Driver's Seat of Your Life?

God knows our tendency to desire control over our own lives. He wants us to replace that desire by letting Jesus assume the driver's seat position of our hearts. It is a much smoother journey when we allow Jesus to take the wheel!

We want our days to play out perfectly, in every way, according to our own definition and sense of direction, but we "all have sinned and fall short of the glory of God" (Rom. 3:23). The position of our steering wheel is slightly skewed to the left because of sin. We need Jesus in the driver's seat to realign our priorities, motives, desires, and tendencies, each day.

We are going to mess up and experience some "mom fails" along the way. Until we allow Christ's strength to fortify our weak areas, we will continue to come up short. But when we allow Jesus' grace to cover us in areas that need His Divine strength and intervention, we experience true success. Paul recounts just this experience in his letter to the Corinthians: "But he said to me, 'My grace is sufficient for you, for my power is made perfect in weakness.' Therefore I will boast all the more gladly about my weaknesses, so that Christ's power may rest on me" (2 Cor. 12:9).

If control is a struggle for you like it is for me, then it is a weakness. Let us surrender the puppet strings of control we hold over our lives and the lives of our children to the Lord in Jesus' Name. We are more than conquerors when we let Jesus take the wheel.

Dear Jesus,

I surrender the control I hold over my heart and life to You. I release the grip I have on my children's lives and allow You to take it, to have full control, to do Your holy work in my children's hearts that only You can do. I trust You, Lord. Thank You, King Jesus, for being in control of every area of my heart. I invite You to take Your rightful place in the driver's seat of my life.

Holy Spirit, please help me in disciplining my children. Help me to be diligent; help me to be heart-focused; help me to be a manager in helping them realize their sin instead of a dictator who commands and condemns. Help me to help them realize there is a better way—Your way.

Holy Spirit, do a work in their hearts. Use me to direct them to follow Your footsteps and choose the righteous path.

In Jesus' Sovereign Name, amen.

Steps of Faith:

- Is there some area of your heart that is closed off to the Lord that you need to reopen and allow the Holy Spirit to have access to? Prayerfully consider this question.

- The book *Don't Make Me Count to Three* by Ginger Hubbard is a great resource that addresses discipline from a Christ-centered perspective. Purchase this book if you would like to dive deeper into what heartfelt, Christ-oriented discipline looks like for parents who are believers.

6
God's Brilliant Love

"Dear friends, let us love one another, for love comes from God. Everyone who loves has been born of God and knows God. Whoever does not love does not know God, because God is love. This is how God showed his love among us: He sent his one and only Son into the world that we might live through him."

1 John 4:7-9

LOVE IS A SIMPLE FOUR-LETTER word with various facets through which light exudes. *Eros* (passionate), *philia* (affectionate), *agape* (sacrificial), *storge* (familial), and *pragma* (enduring) are only five of the many different versions.[1] But what about God's love? God's love is the center stone: the biggest, brightest, most brilliant part of the diamond ring of love. All other stones pale in comparison to God's love for us. It is all-encompassing and incomprehensibly brilliant. It is a stand-alone gem. God's love exceeds and surpasses the standards of the 5 Cs in terms of color, cut, clarity, carat, and certification.

Yes, God's love is engaging and exciting. It is beautiful and bold. His love covers a multitude of sin and shines a bright light into the dark places of our lives (1 Pet. 4:8). God's love is like pure gold, having withstood the test of time through Christ's death, burial, and resurrection, which led to our eternal connection with the Lord God.

---

[1] Elizabeth Rider, "7 Types of Love (And What They Mean)," Elizabeth Rider, Inc., Accessed October 13, 2023, www.elizabethrider.com/7-types-of-love-and-what-they-mean.

Like the formation of a diamond, God's love did not come without much heat and pressure in the form of Christ's earthly trials, but the end product was beyond dazzling. Christ rose from the grave: "He is not here; he has risen, just as he said" (Matt. 28:6). This is the good news.

What joy we can have, and carry with us each day because our Savior lives! He has risen, and His Holy Spirit is alive and available to us—Love in Spirit form. We are to live lives of gratitude because of this precious, sacred gift. We are to walk in God's love and exude it brightly for our children and the world to witness and be blessed by its radiance and warmth.

God's love for us is so great that we get to carry a piece and part of Him inside of our hearts forever. We will experience the magnitude of the Lord's love in full someday, forever in Heaven. This is our reason for hope, our reason for joy, our reason to love and spread the knowledge of God's love to others.

Refuse to shy away from shining God's light. Never snuff out the candle of God's love alive in you. Share it with others. This dark world could use a bright candle like you!

The 5 C's of God's love

Diamonds used for fine jewelry are ranked in terms of five separate standards, known as "the 5 Cs." These standards include cut, color, clarity, carat, and certification.[2] The work of God's love in us can be compared and analyzed through the lens of these diamond standards.

Cut

The cut of a diamond is one of the most important standards to evaluate when selecting a diamond. The proportions and cut of the facets determine how brilliantly that diamond will shine. We too have been cut and shaped as brilliant diamonds the moment we were adopted into the family of God by

2   "The 5 C's of Diamonds (Yes, 5): How to Select the Perfect Engagement Ring," The Natural Diamond Council, July 2, 2020, https://www.naturaldiamonds.com/engagement-rings/how-to-select-the-perfect-engagement-ring.

accepting Christ. The more we learn about Christ's nature and become like Him, the more the facets of our hearts are chiseled and refined to brilliantly reflect Christ's character and God's love.

Color

The color of a diamond ranges on an alphabetical scale from D to Z, D being colorless to Z being a light shade of yellow. When God's love penetrates our hearts, we sparkle and shine. When we accept Jesus into our lives, the Holy Spirit's radiance exudes through us. However, there are certain godly disciplines we can adopt that will make our lives the purest they can be. These disciplines include reading God's Word, prayer, praise and worship, and thanksgiving. Weave these into your life each day for a pure, colorless appeal that pleases the Lord.

Clarity

Clarity refers to blemishes. When we accept Jesus into our hearts, we are forgiven and set free from our sin nature. However, we will continue to sin and fall short of God's glorious standard (Rom. 3:23). One way to eliminate perpetual sin in your life is through accountability. We must bring our sin to light by confessing our transgressions to someone we know, love, and trust, and who is a believer, when that sin seems to fester and grow in darkness. Darkness and light cannot coexist. God's Word tells us, "But everything exposed by the light becomes visible—and everything that is illuminated becomes a light" (Eph. 5:13). Bring your hidden, perpetual sin into the light through confession and accountability. I know it seems daunting, but it will change the conditions of your heart and set you free.

Carat

The fourth C is carat, which refers to the diamond's weight. Oftentimes, carat is confused with the diamond's size, but carat is actually the measure of a diamond's weight. Heavier diamonds are rarer and, therefore, more valuable. When it comes to our faith, it is not the size of our words, deeds, and offerings but, rather, our heart motivations. Do we generously volunteer our time and talent through serving others? Are we cheerful givers? Do we give the Lord one tenth of our earnings, or only what is leftover? Remember that "God loves a cheerful giver" (2 Cor. 9:7).

The Bible story of Cain and Abel (Gen. 4) sheds light onto the topic of giving. The Lord rejected Cain's offering but welcomed Abel's. Abel was shown favor because the offering he brought the Lord was his best, while his brother Cain's sparse offering was rejected. Their offerings were not a reflection of quantity or size but of their motivations and tendencies.

Giving is a form of worship, a way we can tangibly express our love for the Lord. We are simply called to do what we know is right when it comes to generosity. With the Holy Spirit inside of us, we can prayerfully determine how much and when to give. It is not the size of the offering but the eternal weight and value it has in representing the conditions of our hearts and our willingness to obey.

The original twelve disciples left everything they owned and knew and immediately followed after Jesus. Loving and living for God is quite the same. When the Holy Spirit calls us to do something through an act of service, gift, or offering, we are compelled to listen and obey. We are not to question or observe every angle of possibility through hyper-analysis but to say, "Yes, Lord, Your will be done." Our obedience determines the carat factor of God's love and favor present and flowing throughout our lives.

Certification

The last C—certification—is the final factor in diamond classification. It refers to a neutral third-party lab's opinion and stamp mark of approval, verifying the jeweler's classifications. Unlike other faiths, Christianity is not based on works. Our stamp mark of approval can only be found through faith by accepting Jesus as our personal Lord and Savior.

Invitation

There is not a set of requirements to get into Heaven. We simply must accept Jesus as King of our lives and profess that He is Lord. If you have never accepted Jesus into your heart, then I would like to lead you in a prayer to accept the free gift of salvation, which simply means that Jesus will come and live inside of you through His Holy Spirit and will guide, direct, and protect you all of your days. When you accept Jesus into your heart, you are guaranteed everlasting life in Heaven, a place of paradise and eternal connection with God. Are you ready? Pray this prayer out loud. (If you have already accepted Jesus as Lord, state this prayer as a reminder to abide in Christ and remain diligent in faith.)

Dear Jesus,

I confess that I am a sinner in need of a Savior. Forgive me of my sins. Make me a new creation. Jesus, I want You to be the King of my heart and director of my life. I believe that You are the Son of God, that You died on a wooden cross to save me from sin and eternal death, and that You rose again. Jesus, enter into my heart and every facet of my life today. I accept You as my Lord and Savior.

In Jesus' mighty Name I pray, amen.

Congratulations! You have a newfound hope and joy because Jesus is going to guide and guard you all the days of your life. And when those days come to an end, Jesus will welcome you into paradise—a place where there is no death or sorrow, where Jesus will wipe away your every tear (Rev. 21:4). Oh, happy day!

Steps of Faith:

- Share your decision to accept Jesus as King of your life with a trusted friend.
- Read Romans 8 in the Bible.

7
The Transparency of Christ's love and Grace

"And is well known for her good deeds, such as bringing up children, showing hospitality, washing the feet of the Lord's people, helping those in trouble and devoting herself to all kinds of good deeds."

1 Timothy 5:10

IT WAS GETTING DARK OUTSIDE. I was going on a jog to clear my mind from the day's accrued mommy mind fog. When I was almost home, I ran into a neighbor friend who is a mother of three, just like me, but her kids are teenagers. She has been a major blessing to me through reaching out and checking on me periodically, bringing us food after we brought Baby Madison home from the hospital, and volunteering to come over and watch the kids if I ever needed a break. She has been Jesus' hands and feet to me, a demonstration of God's love.

This particular coincidence of running into Heather on my jog brought tears to my eyes and removed something that was hard and unwanted from my heart when she inquired with heartfelt sincerity, "How are you doing? I know it is really hard right now." My kids had been sick the past two weeks, and I had been cooped up and was feeling the weight of being a full-time, relatively new mother of three.

I did not want to cry and was a little surprised myself to feel the heat of hot tears welling up and my face becoming flushed. I was slightly embarrassed. But this woman noticed me. It was like she could see right through my cheerful smile and recognized that I was struggling. She had the arms of her heart stretched out to me and was not just saying a hollow, "How are you doing?" She actually meant it. She went on to inquire, "How can I help you?" When I responded, "I don't know," she went the extra mile to say, "You think on it and let me know."

Part of demonstrating God's love is having a sincere motivation to help others. The mark of Jesus in our lives is the posture of a heart with outstretched arms and hands reaching out to those who may need Jesus' touch. Even if everything appears like peaches and cream on the outside, a person might be in desperate need of a friend and the light of encouragement from Christlike kindness. Always be on the lookout.

What I thought I needed was a quick break, a jog, but this mom's kindness startled me. Her compassion flooded my heart to the point of tears; and while it was slightly embarrassing, I was grateful for her. I was grateful for her love and kindness. I was grateful for her sincerity. I was grateful for the transparency of Jesus in her life. What I needed that day was more than a little fresh air and exercise. What I really needed was a demonstration of God's love, tender mercy, and genuine kindness.

I want to be like Heather someday. I want to wear God's heart on my sleeve. I want the presence of Jesus overflowing from the wellsprings of my heart, pouring out into my life. I want to inspire and uplift other mothers for Jesus.

My neighbor's kindness and love for Jesus blessed me that day. She was truly living out God's second greatest commandment for us as Christ-followers: to love others. While this command is challenging, it is so rewarding. I have a theory that Heather's joy, love, and compassion stems from a blessed heart. Heather is blessed because her kindness and generosity is demonstrated daily through loving others and living for Jesus.

It is easy to lose sight of others as busy mothers, but we must strive to love and help those around us. Someone smiley (or not so smiley) that you know might be desperate for a demonstration of God's love and kindness. Scripture tells us that grace received turns into grace given: "And God is able to bless you abundantly, so that in all things at all times, having all that you need, you will abound in every good work" (2 Cor. 9:8).

I want to be blessed with the measure and fullness of God's all-encompassing love. I must fight against my inwardly-focused tendencies and reach out to a hurting world in need. I must cultivate a mindset and practice of being the hands and feet of Jesus. I must open the eyes of my heart to recognize those in need of Jesus' love and life-saving grace.

Sometimes, God puts people in our path to teach us the meaning of grace in a tangible sense. God's grace is amazing; it is vast and mysterious, wide and deep, full and freeing. God's grace never fails. It continues to amaze me. It trickles in at the most unexpected moments and meets me at my point of need. Paul writes, "He has saved us and called us to a holy life—not because of anything we have done but because of his own purpose and grace. This grace was given us in Christ Jesus before the beginning of time" (2 Tim. 1:9). Praise the Lord for His grace unfolding and covering us with warmth and comfort when we need it most.

A Nice Weight

My antiques business, Heirloom House Antiques, is a part-time gig I enjoy that makes a little extra income for our family. My wonderful mother-in-law was the catalyst for my selling antiques. She has been an antiques dealer for many years and has valuable experience. We paint the town red be-bopping around antique stores when we are together. I always learn something interesting and new. When I am antique shopping with Debbie, occasionally she will pick up an item and say something to the effect of, "It has a nice weight to it." This indicates it is not flimsy, cheap, or made in China.

God's grace carries a nice weight to it. It has the ability to anchor our hearts on relationships that matter. It tethers our souls to the perspective of Christ. God's grace puts wind in our sails and propels our hearts to bless others.

Soften your heart. Let others in. Be a lighthouse for women who are hurting, searching, and seeking Jesus. He wants to use you as a vessel of grace. Your love could be inspirational. Kindness is contagious. Your acts of loving kindness could be the catalyst for someone else to live for the King or to initially accept Jesus for themselves.

Reflect God's brilliant love by blessing others. Love like there's no tomorrow. Allow kindness, generosity, grace, and love to be your legacy. In turn, you will be blessed.

Dear Jesus,

Thank You for being the sacrifice of the world, and for saving a sinner like me. Thank You for being Love Incarnate, for the cross, and for Your resurrection. I praise You for Your great love.

Help me to live a godly life of obedience to Your Word and will, loving my family and all people that I encounter. Help me to shine brightly in this dark world. Help me to brilliantly reflect the love and life You have given me through Your Holy Spirit. Because of what Christ did for me on the cross, may the melody of my life harmonize praise for You.

In Jesus' precious Name, amen.

Steps of Faith:

- Don't shy away. Speak the name of Jesus in conversation today.
- Review 1 Peter 4:8: "Above all, love each other deeply, because love covers over a multitude of sins." In what small way can you show someone God's love today?

Grace to Fill Your Mama Mug

8
The Great Physician

"So we say with confidence, 'The Lord is my helper; I will not be afraid. What can mere mortals do to me?' Remember your leaders, who spoke the word of God to you. Consider the outcome of their way of life and imitate their faith."

Hebrews 13:6-7

WE HAD JUST GOTTEN HOME from a four-night stay at the hospital with our two-year-old daughter, Emma Claire. Our baby girl was sick with pneumonia, and Mommy's heart was worried sick about it. As I watched her sleep our first night back home, I was deeply concerned about her breathing. I had to remind myself, through God's Word, that we have a Great Physician who takes care of our every need and the needs of our children. Through prayer, I reoriented the arrow of my worried heart to point away from myself and my immediate circumstances and instead look upward in the direction of God Who is ultimately, in a word, "good." I knew that the Lord was in command. He was going to watch over, heal, and restore my daughter's breathing and lungs in His way and timing.

There have been many times throughout the course of motherhood that my mommy heart has been left in shambles, my anxiety levels spiked sky high. But when I get into God's Word, I am reminded of where my help comes from. My heart rests assured, and my mind trusts in God's healing, almighty power through His Divine Word. Through the Scriptures, I am reminded that the resurrected King has the ability to resurrect and restore my broken-down situations.

The Great Physician heals us whenever our hearts worry. He cares for us when we need an extra helping of hope. He prescribes us with His goodness, peace, and love, according to our every need. We have to believe that our God is mighty to save when our children are sick or going through unideal circumstances. God's incalculable love covers our anxious hearts. Philippians 4:6-7 states, "Do not be anxious about anything, but in every situation, by prayer and petition, with thanksgiving, present your requests to God. And the peace of God, which transcends all understanding, will guard your hearts and your minds in Christ Jesus." I love the fact that the peace of Jesus' presence trumps our knowledge and perspective of earthly affairs. God's love encapsulates our worried minds, hopes, and fears.

It is so easy to worry about our children, but worry is not from God. What is from God is peace. What God provides is hope. What God wants to give each and every one of us is lasting joy that surpasses our circumstances. Through prayerful supplication, the Holy Spirit can encompass our fears, encapsulate our despondency, and replace our tears with laughter and singing. We can be like the woman described in Proverbs: "She is clothed with strength and dignity; she can laugh at the days to come" (Prov. 31:25).

When our hearts cry out for help and our souls are burdened beyond what we can bear, may we seek the Author and Perfecter of our faith, Jesus Christ. Our worries, fears, and negative thoughts can be turned into joy and gratitude that delves beyond our day-to-day life scenarios when Christ is the Strength of our souls.

Trading Anxiety for Christ's Peace

The Bible story of two sisters, Mary and Martha, depicts a worried Martha who is more concerned about the housework, chores, and to-do list than listening to Jesus. She places her worry over time spent with the Lord, and she is rebuked because of it. Jesus says to her, "'You are worried and upset about many things, but few things are needed—or indeed only one. Mary has chosen what is better, and it will not be taken away from her'" (Luke 10:41-42).

Let us choose Jesus before our worries and to-do lists. He wants to hear from our hearts first. Before your husband, friends, and family members, prioritize speaking to Jesus and sharing the worries of your heart with the Great Physician. He alone has the ability to heal, restore, and rid your mind of all fear and anxiety.

In terms of anxiety, I am not discounting the power of counselors and doctors; I am simply recommending that you seek Jesus first. The Lord instilled doctors and counselors with knowledge and wisdom to aid patients in need of medicine and wise counsel. When you are worried about your kids, life circumstances, or other afflictions that come along with the role of "Mama," realize that God has got you; but He may want to help you through counseling or medicine.

There is no pit too deep that our Heavenly Father cannot get to. There is no mountain too tall, no river too wide, no road too long. Jesus will leave the ninety-nine to come and find you. Call out His name. Speak the name of Jesus. Let the Lord come and rescue you from whatever worry is weighing on your mama heart today.

The best thing to do when you are worried or in a place of uncertainty is to seek Jesus in prayer and through God's Word. Turn on some Christian worship music and open your Bible. Turn down your radio in the car and simply talk to God. I know that being a mom is so demanding, but try to carve out some time for your Lord and Savior each day. Make it a priority. Allow Christ's peace to guard your heart and mind.

First Peter 3:11 says we must "seek peace and pursue it." Jesus is the Peace we so desperately long for. We must pursue Jesus so that His peace can seal our minds with the sacred power of His holy presence. Jesus' presence changes everything. The powerful presence of Jesus can give the blind sight. It can enable the lame to walk and run. It can heal our sick babies. It can overpower our worried hearts. It can exchange our daily struggles with victory.

In Jesus' name, surrender your worries to the Lord, Who is mighty to forgive, heal, exchange, and restore. Pour out your heart. "Cast all your anxiety on him because he cares for you" (1 Pet. 5:7). Let His prescription of love, joy, peace, and hope fill your heart in full.

Dear Jesus,

We love You, and we need You. We love the way You hold us through our trials. We seek after the peace of Your presence. We long for the joy of Your embrace.

May Your love cover us. We need Your peace to envelop our anxious hearts. We trade in our worries for the calmness we experience in Your green pastures near your quiet streams (Ps. 23). Your peace transcends all knowledge and understanding (Phil. 4:7).

Thank You for the peace of Your presence, which covers our fears. Please be our Strength when we feel weak, worried, and anxious. Fortify our hearts and replace our fears with faith. We trade in our worry for Your hope. Rearrange our doubts and discouragement to be fully encompassed by Your all-consuming love.

Thank You, God, for Your great love in sending us Your Son. Thank You for the healing resurrection power of Jesus in our lives.

In Jesus' wonderful Name, amen.

Steps of Faith:

- What are your worries, fears, and weaknesses? Prayerfully confess these things to God. Ask Jesus to ladle His peace over your mind, His presence over your fears, and His strength over your weaknesses.
- Dwell on this verse as a prayer. Keep it on the forefront of your mind throughout the day: "The LORD is my light and my

salvation—whom shall I fear? The LORD is the stronghold of my life—of whom shall I be afraid?" (Ps. 27:1).

- Is there anything weighing down your mama heart today? Approach God in prayer and tell Him your concerns. Ask Him to step into the situation and give you peace and answers throughout the day.

9
He Is for You

"And we know that in all things God works for the good of those who love him,
who have been called according to his purpose."

Romans 8:28

SOME MOMENTS OF MOTHERHOOD ARE more difficult than others. Some days are difficult physically. Some days are difficult emotionally. Some days are difficult both physically and emotionally! Some seasons of motherhood require every last ounce of strength running through our bodies. When we are outgunned, outnumbered, and overwhelmed by our children's needs, inquiries, and behaviors, the odds feel stacked against us. But we serve a God who is *for* us. He can be our strength when we have nothing left to give.

In the same way that Jesus multiplied the fishes and loaves the boy had to offer at the Sermon on the Mount, Jesus can give us His Divine ability to overcome the daily struggle and conquer our anxious thoughts. When we come to Jesus with what we have, no matter how small our heart-offering, Jesus can multiply our portions.

Romans 8:28 gives us a promise. It gives us hope. Even when the going gets rough, God's presence never leaves or forsakes us. Even though some days are difficult, Jesus paid it all so that we could have assurance of life to the fullest. As Christ-followers, we are daily connected with God. This is a gift in and of itself. Let's reach out to Jesus and ask Him to be our steady Strength.

God is working on our behalf. He is orchestrating our lives behind the scenes. Even when we cannot see it, God's plans are good. He works in our favor. His ways are perfect, even when the struggle is real.

God has positioned you in your home, with your spouse, as the mother of your children for a reason. Lean into this truth through moments of struggle. When God's purposes seem to be surrounded by a sea of fog, push past the dim and recognize the light. Ask God to guide you through dark days and enable you to mother from the strength of His might.

God wants to use you in miraculous ways, Mama! Say yes. Step forward in faith. Move toward the light in your life. Choose to fight for the Lord's plans to unfold in your home. Refuse to shrink back in fear. With the Spirit of the living God inside of us, there is nothing that we cannot accomplish. No mountain is too big; no task He asks of us is too small. God's power, authority, and holy presence trumps all. We serve a God so big, Whose greatness stretches beyond our understanding. And still, He cares about the little details of our lives. He so dearly cares. He stepped down from Heaven to fulfill our desperate need. He is *for* you.

Blessed Assurance

Jesus came to earth and confronted every trial, feeling, fear, and emotion we will ever encounter at its root. We can approach His presence with confidence because we are assured of His mercy and grace. In the places that we need it most, Jesus is able to apply His healing balm of peace, which comes from His presence when we seek Him.

Motherhood is challenging. Life is tough. Some waves carry more momentum and crash over us with brute force, while others seem more tolerable but are more repetitive, wearing us down all the same. No one gets a free pass from the darts of hardship life throws. But what we do get, as women of faith, is the blessed assurance that God is going to be with us.

In whatever you face today, lean into Jesus' grace, mercy, and love. Seek His face and you will find kindness and compassion in full. Look into His eyes, and you will discover a sea of unconditional love and unharnessed peace. It will flood your heart, mind, and soul. It will unveil the truth that the glory of God is in you. You do have the strength to stand. In whatever it is you are going through, seek His face for the life-giving support you so desperately need. Jesus loves you—flaws, fears, failures, and all. What blessed assurance we have because of Jesus' righteous blood.

Thank you, Jesus, for forgiveness. Thank You for finding me and drawing me out from the dark places where I tend to hide. Thank You for Your illuminating truth that proclaims the promise: You are with me. You are for me. You have already gone before me.

You're Gonna Miss This

As a new mom, I struggled with letting go of my former life, undoing the focus on me, and reorienting the focus of my life to be on my family. It was a daily struggle, but the Lord led me through it and has taught me so much along the way. The transition of becoming a stay-at-home mom and wife was a humbling experience that made me depend on Jesus and rediscover the fact that my identity is rooted in Christ alone.

I went from being a full-time elementary school teacher to staying at home full time with a brand-new baby. I can remember breastfeeding that tiny baby, reciting Scripture, reading books, and trying not to lose my mind. Being a stay-at-home mom was a huge blessing, no doubt, but it was a change of pace that put my twenty-seven-year-old self into a state of shock, like jumping into an icy cold swimming pool without knowing what the water would be like.

Before having a baby, I watched other mamas with their newborns, thinking how blissful motherhood must be. I could not wait to have a baby of my own! I did not realize any of the behind-the-scenes work and nonstop dedication that having a new baby would require.

At the time, I knew that I should be extremely grateful to be able to stay at home, and I was. But that did not make the challenge of transitioning into this new way of a much quieter, less-structured lifestyle any easier. Eventually, my husband and I had another baby, and then another. The pace has definitely picked up around here! I have grown to love what I do, but I will never forget those early days of being a brand-new mom.

By leaning into God's Word and getting involved in a Bible study, joining the organization MOPS (Mothers of Preschoolers), making the decision to attempt to become a good cook, and praying for my husband and family each day, the Lord was able to refine me. I still struggle when it comes to the "me" vs. "we" concept of laying down my life each day to serve my family, but my love for motherhood has grown. Like a snowball effect, I love being called "Mama," and there is no stopping the speed and growth of this snowball. My love for my children becomes greater each day. My enjoyment of being a stay-at-home mom continues to increase. In blessing the lives of others, we, in turn, become blessed. Being a stay-at-home mom has become one of the greatest gifts and blessings to me.

In reaching out and establishing relationships with other Christian mamas who had similar daily struggles, I was able to learn from, relate to, and become more grateful for my life in being able to stay at home as a mom. Some days are tough; but overall, these days are so precious, and I know they will not last.

I try to place myself in the shoes of an older version of myself when I feel discouraged. Potty training accidents, mammoth-sized messes, constant business—I realize that these things are small potatoes. When I become frustrated or overwhelmed, I take a step back and choose to listen to the country song by Trace Adkins playing in my mind, "You're Gonna Miss This." The song actually makes me sad because I know it is true.

Someday, I am going to want this sweet and innocent stage back. But over sadness, it brings me hope and joy for today. I am encouraged in knowing that my children will put on their own clothes someday, they will entertain themselves more often, they will poo-poo in the potty ten times out of ten. I keep reminding myself of this simple yet profound truth: everyone gets potty-trained eventually. It puts the little (or not so little) messes in perspective of a much bigger picture.

I will miss this stage. I will miss this precious season of sticky fingers, open mouth kisses, and "I wub yous." I will want these years of wiping away tears, kissing boo-boos, sharing unharnessed laughter, pushing swings, and enjoying pure innocence back. Like the sands of time, the days keep slipping through my fingers. I will never get to relive these sweet moments, but I will forever treasure their memories.

Sometimes, I like to imagine what it will be like when my kids are all grown and we are sitting around the table at Thanksgiving, enjoying each other's company. Thoughts like this keep me going. Sweet little things my toddlers say also give me joy for the day.

I recorded a prayer that Emma Claire recently said because I want to relive it and relish her sweet three-year-old soul: "Dear Jesus, thank You for buying our food. Thank You for building our house! Thank You for . . . bless these flowers. Thank You for dying in me on the cross. In Jeeeeesus' Name, amen."

In the thick and thin moments of motherhood, Jesus has got you, Mama. I know it can be tough, but it is all going to be okay. *I promise.* Try to enjoy this season you are in because it simply will not last.

Many moms choose to "whiteout" the busy years. They remember the way that their struggles with their toddlers made them feel. Therefore, they choose to forget the little details rather than cherish them. I want to remember so that I remember to give God glory for getting me through it. Being a mom of littles is not a slice of cheesecake, but we can learn to enjoy the bumpy ride. We can look back, remember the potholes and joys along the way, and say with full confidence, "God made a way." He always does, and He forever will provide for our every need.

There is an assortment of monuments and memorials to be found in the Bible that served the purpose of helping biblical characters remember the Lord God. The very first monument was erected by Jacob after having a prophetic dream. As a form of worship and praise, he consecrated the stone on which he slept (Gen. 28:10-22). Another monument of sorts that we practice today is the Lord's Supper. We take the elements of bread and wine or grape juice in remembrance of Jesus. The cross, too, is a memorial that we often wear around our necks, wrists, or fingers and hang up in our homes that is symbolic to all that Christ accomplished through His crucifixion on the hill of Golgotha.

Let's not take for granted all that Jesus went through to pave a way for us to receive eternal life. Let's not take for granted motherhood—one of life's greatest blessings—that also has some incredibly challenging moments. The next time your toddler flushes toys down the toilet or decides to play in the dog's poop—or worse—remind yourself that these things are small potatoes. Someday, you will look back and laugh at it all. You will long to relive these sweet little years. So do not take a single second for granted. You may not see it now, but "you're gonna miss this."

> *Dear Jesus,*
>
> *Thank You for my children. Thank You for what a blessing they are to me. Help me to be a blessing as a mother in their lives. Remind me to be thankful for the day and grateful for every little moment, even the hiccups along the way.*
>
> *Instill in me an understanding that these days of motherhood are slowly slipping away. Help me to enjoy my children and love being a mom. Remind me that the joy is in the journey of motherhood, not the getting there. Help me to be faithful in loving my family each day.*

Jesus, help me to be the best mom that I can be. Show me ways that I can live more diligently and faithfully for You alone.

In Jesus' holy Name, amen.

Steps of Faith:

- Count your blessings! Think of five blessings that you are grateful for, record them, and thank Jesus for those things.
- Start jotting down little things your children say that warm your heart and put them in a jar, keep them in a notebook, or make a note on your phone.
- Listen to the country song, "You're Gonna Miss This" by Trace Adkins. Ask God to step in and give you joy and contentment through this season.

10
Two Little Pink Lines

"Children are a heritage from the Lord, offspring a reward from him. Like arrows in the hands of a warrior are children born in one's youth. Blessed is the man whose quiver is full of them. They will not be put to shame when they contend with their opponents in court."

Psalm 127:3-5

HOW CAN TWO LITTLE PINK lines hold so much meaning? Responsibility, lifelong love, incredible joy, and Christ's faithfulness—the two little pink lines staring back at me spoke of all these things and more.

When we found out I was pregnant with our third baby, I had some mixed emotions. We knew we wanted a third child, but I did not realize how quickly the Lord would bless us with baby number three! We already had a two-year-old and a one-year-old in tow and were feeling a bit starstruck pondering the arrival of a third baby.

Looking around, I felt like my housekeeping skills were lacking, my house littered with toys and breadcrumbs scattered across the floor. I felt behind in terms of laundry, housework, and running my antiques business. I felt like a failure in the kitchen because my kids were often too busy for me to be able to cook dinners. I felt alone at times.

All of the lies began to add up in my mind, until I heard a small but sure voice speak over the condemnation, "Stop! Now take another look." I noticed that my children were happy and well-fed. I remembered that my husband loves me dearly. The dog's bowl had food in it. The Bible on my desk was evidence that a quiet time had taken place that day.

It was brought to my attention that my heart is content in Christ alone. My success is not measured by a beautiful home, an orderly life, or my fleeting feelings, but rather a life of godliness that is grace-filled, edifying to others, and pleasing to the Lord. His Word reminds me, "His divine power has given us everything we need for a godly life through our knowledge of him who called us by his own glory and goodness" (2 Pet. 1:3).

I realized then and there that God was going to equip me and my husband for the challenge of having three babies, ages three and under. I knew it was going to be a *major* challenge. But I knew with absolute certainty that God was going to be my Portion and Strength throughout it all (Psalm 73:26). Second Peter 1:3 assured me that the Lord would infuse me with His Divine omnipotence, equip me with His righteousness, and fortify the strength of my soul with His power and presence. Infuse, equip, fortify, empower—*yes*, God would do these things in me.

I knew that being a mom and having a third baby was an assignment the Lord had called me to. Because I had been called by Jesus, I knew that I would also be equipped by Jesus. The Lord would give me all that I needed to live a godly life and care for my children. I had less to worry about and more to celebrate in knowing that the Holy Spirit would help my children come to know Jesus and equip me to aid them in their walks of faith.

With a new perspective of grace for myself and an "I can" attitude provided by the Holy Spirit, I was overjoyed in looking forward to experiencing God's love in flesh form. Children are a blessing, "a heritage from the Lord" (Ps. 127:3).

Have you ever read the children's story *The Mitten*? A little boy loses his mitten; and while he is looking for it, several animals come and find their home inside of the mitten, one after the other. A mouse, a hedgehog, a badger, a fox, a snowy owl, and a bear all burrow their way inside of the mitten to stay sheltered from the winter storm. The mitten expands and provides shelter and warmth to all of these creatures, all at once.[3] In the same way, God has the Divine ability to widen the diameter of all that our arms can hold when our hearts are open and ready to do His will. This includes raising and loving a tribe of children.

When our hands are lifted up and ready to accept God's Divine assignments, God will give us the strength and all that we need to equip us to carry out His will. We may have to get a little uncomfortable at times and even forfeit some of our creature comforts, but God will step in and be our daily strength. When we seek to do the Lord's will in life, God is able to grow our faith, which is a tremendous blessing in and of itself. Whether it is having more children or some other assignment, say yes. God is going to equip and empower you.

Dear Jesus,

Thank You for my children. Thank You for what a daily blessing they are in my life. Thank You for entrusting them to my care. Help me to lead them to You and provide them with an arrow that points to You each and every day. Thank You, Jesus, for Your strength. Thank You for Divinely providing me with the fortification I need on a daily basis to raise my children.

Holy Spirit, use me as a vessel and intercede in my children's lives. Help me show them Your love and lead them to You and Your heart. May they find solace sitting at Your feet, King Jesus. Reveal to me Your will. Place assignments in my life and grow my faith in accepting and carrying out Your plans and Kingdom-purposes. Embolden me. Teach me to live unhindered, undaunted, and unashamedly for You.

Thank You for Your Divine provision and ability to expand my arms and heart to carry all that You have for me.

In Jesus' heavenly Name, amen.

---

3   Jan Brett, *The Mitten* (New York: G. P. Putnam's Sons, 1989).

Steps of Faith:

- Read the story *The Mitten* to your children today or listen to the story online. Reflect on the faithfulness of the Lord in providing us with the strength and endurance that we need each day to love and care for our children.

11
Overcoming the Daily Struggle

"'So do not fear, for I am with you; do not be dismayed, for I am your God. I will strengthen you and help you; I will uphold you with my righteous right hand.'"

Isaiah 41:10

DO YOU EVER FEEL OVERWHELMED in motherhood? Like perhaps you were not cut out for this mom gig? I do at times! I want you to know that you are not alone in your feelings of inadequacy. God wants to meet us in the middle of our struggles and shortcomings and cover us with His perfect grace.

In motherhood and in life, the Lord gives us all that we need. David writes in Psalms, "The Lord is my shepherd; I lack nothing" (Ps. 23:1). Why do you think the psalmist was stating these words? Was it because he was beaming with confidence? Nope! He was overwhelmed, anxiety-ridden, and afraid. David was writing this psalm as a steady reminder that the Lord God is our Shepherd. He protects and provides all that we need. He is our heart's Portion and daily Strength (Ps. 73:26).

We can be grateful because although we may feel overwhelmed at times, God gives us exactly what we need—all the time. The good news is that we have the Holy Spirit to guide us along life's way. Jesus is our Strength and Strong Tower (Prov. 18:10). Jesus is our Portion and Daily Bread (Matt. 6:11). Jesus is our Rock and Firm Foundation (Ps. 18). Jesus is our Hope stored up in "jars of clay" (2 Cor. 4:7). God's Word fills us with hope, saying, "Therefore we do not lose heart. Though outwardly we are wasting away, yet inwardly we are being renewed day by day. For our light and momentary troubles are achieving for us an eternal glory that far outweighs them all. So we fix our eyes not on what is seen, but on what is unseen, since what is seen is temporary, but what is unseen is eternal" (2 Cor. 4:16-18).

As moms, we might feel like we are living on a shoestring budget, in terms of having margin and free time; but we are doing God's holy work, ladies! Do not lose sight of that fact. Motherhood is such a precious sacrifice that we can be grateful for because God is sanctifying us throughout the process of leading and helping our little children become strong, Christ-equipped people. We are raising up warriors—men and women who will know, love, and live for Jesus, leading others to the cross along the way. Do not lose sight of what a wonderful sacrifice it is that you are making in raising up your children for the Lord.

The Lord goes before us in motherhood and in life. He paves a way and perfectly provides for our every need and those of our children. The Lord God is mighty to uphold the shoestrings of our lives with the chain of His strength. We have got this because God has got us! Do not lose heart.

Some days do not feel like rainbows and sunshine. Some days are hard—really hard—not the kind of hard that jellybeans get in the cold but the kind of hard the frozen Arctic tundra becomes in the wintertime. Wearing all the hats that being a mom entails can be a struggle, but I know that the Lord is my Strength and my Portion (Ps. 73:26), the place where my help comes from (Ps. 121:1).

God has got us, even on days that feel overwhelming, overbearing, and overdone. When we feel burned out and cry out to Jesus, He can sustain our minds and be the strength our hearts need. The truth is that being a mom is no cake walk, and there are going to be days that we feel like we just can't. On those days, in those moments of desperation, cry out to Jesus. Let Him be all that you need. Lean into the Lord through prayer. Ask for His love, wisdom, comfort, and support to hold you up and enable you to stand. Through stretches of wilderness seasons, silence, and unanswered prayers, press into Jesus.

There is a woman in the Bible who did just this. If we look at the life of Hannah, we will find an example of unwavering faith. (Read 1 Samuel 1). Hannah longed for a child. She prayed without ceasing. She leaned into the Lord through prayer, until her prayer was finally answered.

Hannah's faith astounds me, and I believe she deserves a standing ovation. Hannah prayed for *years*. Although your prayer might not be for a baby, maybe it is for a life circumstance to change, for a blessing to be delivered, for a wayward child or relative to return to the Lord, for your boss to notice your hard work and promote you, for freedom from debt, for your marriage to be restored, or for your heart to be healed. Whatever desperate prayer you harbor in your heart, cry out to Jesus. Let Him be the Source of your steady strength. Refuse to surrender. Stand strong through the storm. Remain fervent in prayer. Lean into Jesus through this wilderness season, for the Lord is fortifying your faith and equipping you with the endurance to run your race with perseverance. As Romans 5:3-5 reminds us, "Not only so, but we also glory in our sufferings, because we know that suffering produces perseverance; perseverance, character; and character, hope. And hope does not put us to shame, because God's love has been poured out into our hearts through the Holy Spirit, who has been given to us."

Lean in. Lean into Jesus. Lean into Jesus with all your might. Pray. Pray fervently, pray diligently, and pray passionately. Pray with an expectant heart. Know that the Lord hears your cry and is going to answer whatever prayer you pray in His perfect timing, in His perfect way. We know this to be true because the God we serve is ultimately good. He is faithful. He is true. His plans never bring harm but always help and lead us into a glistening hope and a sun-soaked future (Jer. 29:11). Lean in.

New Morning Mercies

It was a gloomy day, and I felt like a complete failure as a mom. I had lost my cool and raised my voice when disciplining one of my children. My husband and I got into an argument in front of the kids. I failed to read my Bible that day. I did not read to my children from their children's Bible either. I did not even get a chance to brush my teeth. Instead of drawing from a well of gratitude, I was hitting rock bottom, coming up empty, and acting grouchy because of it. I felt like Alexander from *Alexander and the Terrible, Horrible No Good, Very Bad Day,* and I really do not care for that book. It had been a tough day.

The next day, I was driving my kids home from Mother's Day Out when I heard my three-year-old whisper, "Jesus." She was saying it in an endearing sort of way. Through that crack the Holy Spirit gave me, I could see Jesus' light shining through that little girl. It was a window of opportunity, and I was able to tell my toddlers sitting in the backseat why we love Jesus and explain to them the "bigness" of God's love.

My rendition of the Gospel was far from perfect, but I knew that I needed to feed the Word of God to my children's hungry, little souls at that moment. Our children are naturally inquisitive about Jesus because of the Holy Spirit's promptings taking place in their hearts. It does not have to be perfect, or anywhere close, but pray that the Holy Spirit would give you opportunities to talk about Jesus and the right words to say. The Lord has entrusted you with the precious little souls of your children. Feed them well.

Hebrews 4:14-16 paints a beautiful picture of the grace available to us in Christ:

> Therefore, since we have a great high priest who has ascended into heaven, Jesus the Son of God, let us hold firmly to the faith we profess. For we do not have a high priest who is unable to empathize with our weaknesses, but we have one who has been tempted in every way, just as we are—yet he did not sin. Let us then approach God's throne of grace with confidence,

so that we may receive mercy and find grace to help us in our time of need.

There is grace for us in motherhood because of what Jesus accomplished on the cross. The world shouts, "Be perfect!" "You are not doing it right unless your kids are eating gourmet, organic food at all times!" "You failed today, and that equates you to a failure." "You will never measure up!" But the Lord tells us something quite contrary to popular opinion: "My grace is sufficient for you" (2 Cor. 12:9). You do not have to be the perfect mom. Just do your best and keep putting one foot in front of the other. Rely on the Lord's sunshine and grace in your life on days that feel dark, drab, and despondent. Get into God's Word. Go to Him in prayer. Rely on His mercy. Rely on His truth. Rely on Jesus' great love to carry you.

Whisper this little prayer: "Lord, I need You now. Be my daily strength. Holy Spirit, surround me on all sides of my life. Today, I trade in my worry, anxiety, and overwhelmed mind for *Your* love, *Your* peace, *Your* power, and *Your* protection. Establish the stronghold of Your roots in me. In Jesus' powerful Name, amen."

In motherhood, some days are more difficult than others; but through Christ Jesus, there are new mercies for us each and every day. God is faithful to forgive. He is faithful to offer us freedom from our sins and former mom failures because He sent His only Son to be condemned on our behalf and save us. We have hope because of Jesus. Hope for tomorrow, hope to get us through today, hope in the unideal circumstances, hope in the waiting, hope for the unseen, hope in the everlasting—all because of Jesus. In the words of Jeremiah the prophet, "I remember my affliction and my wandering, the bitterness and the gall. I well remember them, and my soul is downcast within me. Yet this I call to mind and therefore I have hope: Because of the Lord's great love we are not consumed, for his compassions never fail. They are new every morning; great is your faithfulness" (Lam. 3:19-23).

Dear Jesus,

Please be my strength. Sometimes I get overwhelmed. My heart gets flooded with fluctuating emotions and discouragement creeps in. Please step in and stop the rising tide. Remind me of Your grace in my moments of weakness and doubt. Be the light of my life through prayer on days that feel dark. Provide the spark for a fire through Your Word when the world around me gets chilly.

What a wonderful privilege it is to have children, to be able to shepherd the little ones of Your Kingdom. Help me to do Your holy work daily in raising up my children to know and love You. Help me not lose sight of all that I am doing to honor You in the process of motherhood. Remind me of how worthy of a task it is to be a mom. Fill me with Your humility, grace, and compassion. Help me to be sensitive to Your Holy Spirit. Show me ways that I can honor you daily.

God, I need Your love and grace to cover me, to encompass my struggles, to encapsulate my worried mind, to envelop my anxious heart. Jesus, I need You. Come into my life. Be my daily Strength. Let the peace of Your presence calm my anxiousness and fill me to the brim.

Thank You, Jesus, for the privilege and honor of being called "mommy." I know I do not say this often enough: Thank You for my children. Thank You for Your grace in this grand endeavor of raising the little ones of Your Kingdom. Empower, equip, and embolden me.

In Jesus' holy Name, amen.

Steps of Faith:

- Is there anything that you need to seek the Lord's mercy and forgiveness for? Ask the Lord to search your heart. Pray for His new mercies to cover and carry you today!

- Speak these words of truth and encouragement over your life: "Because of the grace, guidance, and goodness of Jesus, I am a terrific mama! I am doing the Lord's holy work in raising up men and women who know and love the Lord. I am trying my best, and God honors my efforts. He walks alongside me down this topsy-turvy, grace-filled, glorious, windy, wild, and beautiful road of motherhood."

12
So long, loneliness!

"'The days are coming,' declares the Lord, 'when I will make a new covenant with the people of Israel and with the people of Judah . . . This is the covenant that I will make with the house of Israel after that time,' declares the Lord. 'I will put my law in their minds and write it on their hearts. I will be their God, and they will be my people.'"

Jeremiah 31:31, 33

DO YOU EVER FEEL LONELINESS ooze into your life like toothpaste being opened after a high-altitude flight? I do sometimes! Although you might feel alone, you are not. There are so many other moms who think and feel exactly the same way you do. We are in the same boat, Mama! Do not let the enemy try to tell you otherwise.

One year, I decided at the last minute to go to the If Gathering. I could not find anyone to go with me so late in the game and went by myself. I sat there in the church pew, by myself, while other ladies chatted and conversed freely. I felt utterly alone. Then I saw a lady with whom I attended church and struck up a conversation. I had to take the first step, but there was somebody else out there in the same boat, someone who needed a friend.

Be that friend, Mama! I cannot tell you how thrilled another mother will be when you reach out to her. Recently, I was on the receiving end of a mother reaching out to me. It was such a pleasant surprise and unique blessing. Do not wait for someone to reach out to you. Simply ask for that acquaintance's number and say, "We should get together sometime!" Suggest a time and place to meet. Maybe it is a playdate, meeting at a coffee shop on a Saturday morning, or taking a walk; do not give up on making friends. This is how we fulfill the command of Scripture: "And let us consider how we may spur one another on toward love and good deeds, not giving up meeting together, as some are in the habit of doing, but encouraging one another—and all the more as you see the Day approaching" (Heb. 10:24-25).

With Us Always

Matthew 28:20 is the very last verse of the book of Matthew. Jesus says, "'And teaching them to obey everything I have commanded you. And surely I am with you always, to the very end of the age.'" Jesus stated these final parting words right after proclaiming the Great Commission. Such profound assurance these words provide. Jesus is with us *always.*

The disciples were Jesus' beloved friends. They had done ministry alongside Him for approximately three years and were very close. They had witnessed the miracles. They had broken bread with, walked alongside, and gleaned so much wisdom from their Lord, Savior, and Friend. They were going to miss Jesus, indeed. But Jesus assured them that He would be with them always, and He gives us this same promise today.

Because we are disciples of Jesus, God is with us through His Holy Spirit. Jesus Christ resides in our hearts, and there is nothing we have to do to earn His presence. Can we reach a greater degree of closeness to the Lord when we live by faith and abide in God's will through steadfast obedience? I believe so. But because of God's love and grace, we have the free gift of salvation, the Holy Spirit in our hearts. Jesus is with us, forever and always. David writes of this comfort in Psalm 23:4: "Even though I walk through the darkest valley, I will fear no evil, for you are with me; your rod and your staff, they comfort me."

The definition of being "alone" indicates that no one else is present. As moms, we constantly have the presence of little ones surrounding us. But in motherhood, it is possible to experience loneliness without being alone. We might feel lonely at times throughout the ever-changing seasons of motherhood and life, but the Lord is ever-present. Even when we do not feel Jesus' presence, He is still there. First Peter 5:7 says, "Cast all your anxiety on him because he cares for you." This verse assures our hearts that Jesus is always here for us.

Through the thick and thin slices of motherhood and life, Jesus wants to be our Daily Bread. He wants us to reach out our hands to Him so that He can hold them within His own. He wants to lead us. He wants to be our steady Strength. He wants us to recognize Him as the Source of our power, where our help comes from (Ps. 121:1). As He said through the prophet Jeremiah, "'Then you will call on me and come and pray to me, and I will listen to you. You will seek me and find me when you seek me with all your heart'" (Jer. 29:12-13).

On days when you well up with worry and feel alone in your struggles, rest assured that the power and grace of the Lord covers you. Allow His blanket of love and compassion to fully encompass your mind, anxieties, fears, and feelings of loneliness. Although you may feel lonely, you are never alone with the Holy Spirit inside of you.

Dear Jesus,

Thank You for Your holy presence in my life. Help me to fight feelings of loneliness with Your truth and the knowledge of Your ever-flowing grace and presence. Replace my loneliness with joy that comes from knowing and loving You. I pray that You would fill my life in full.

Help me to rely on You in moments of uncertainty, on days that are painted blue. Help me to seek You through seasons of abundance and drought. Lord, You are my Portion, my Strong Tower, and Best Friend.

I pray that I would be a lighthouse to other mothers, a station where warmth and friendship can be found. Strengthen my arms to be outreaching. Point out women who need a friend, and lead me to be that light in their lives.

Give me sensitivity to Your Spirit. Give me ears to walk in tune with Your presence. Give me discernment to follow Your lead and depend on You for daily comfort, peace, and love. Thank You for being with me, forever and always.

In Jesus' holy Name, amen.

Steps of Faith:

- Reach out to another mama today. Text an acquaintance or a friend and schedule a playdate or a time to go get coffee and chat. There are other mamas out there who feel alone. Do not be afraid to take the first steps toward friendship.

- Replace your loneliness with God's truth. Review the following verses:
  - "'So do not fear, for I am with you; do not be dismayed, for I am your God. I will strengthen you and help you; I will uphold you with my righteous right hand'" (Is. 41:10).
  - "He heals the brokenhearted and binds up their wounds" (Ps. 147:3).
  - "A father to the fatherless, a defender of widows, is God in his holy dwelling. God sets the lonely in families, he leads out the prisoners with singing; but the rebellious live in a sun-scorched land" (Ps. 68:5-6).
  - "Surely, Lord, you bless the righteous; you surround them with your favor as with a shield" (Ps. 5:12).

- Spend at least five minutes with Jesus in prayer today. Talk to Him out loud if you can. Set a timer if you need to. Know that you are not alone because the powerful presence of our Lord and Savior illuminates our lives.

13
Grace Over Perfection

"But you are a chosen people, a royal priesthood, a holy nation, God's special possession, that you may declare the praises of him who called you out of darkness into his wonderful light."

1 Peter 2:9

I USED TO CARE MORE about folding the laundry than getting into God's Word. I used to try to clean every last dish in the sink before bowing my head in prayer. I used to want all of the toys on the floor and clutter on the countertops removed before examining the clutter and mess that was inside of my heart. I used to strive for outward perfection while neglecting my spiritual well-being, the conditions of my heart.

Externally, everything was perfect; but on the inside, my soul was crying out, desperate for Jesus. Eventually, all of my perfectionist tendencies caught up with me, and the Lord broke me. I had an epiphany moment in the form of unexpected, unwarranted, unstoppable tears over something very minor that caused me to pause long enough to pray and realize that I could not win the perfection game no matter how hard I tried.

Perfection is a mirage, something we will never be able to attain, no matter how determined we are to reach it. By the time we catch up with it, the scenery will have changed. Like the image of a ship sailing upside down on the ocean horizon, or a pool of water on the sun-scorched road up ahead, perfection will always be just out of our reach. Striving for it will only leave us feeling empty inside.

By joining a Bible study and getting into God's Word and through prayer, the Lord was able to pull me out of the trap of perfection I was ensnared in. Although my to-do list was not always wiped clean by the end of each day, God blanketed me with His love. He covered me with His plush grace. Resting in God's benevolence was such a relief, like a much-needed siesta, a hard-earned sabbatical, or a sunny spring hike after a long, harsh winter.

To His chosen people, God says, "In repentance and rest is your salvation, in quietness and trust is your strength, but you would have none of it'" (Isa. 30:15). Like a ray of sunshine, the Lord's presence in my life radiated warmth and became recognizable as ripe apples began to grow. These apples were love, joy, peace, patience, kindness, goodness, faithfulness, gentleness, and self-control. These fruits stemmed from the Tree of Life, Jesus in me.

You cannot be a perfect mom. Make the cognizant decision to stop running and training for the perfect mom race. I know this is contrary to popular opinion; but as Christ-followers, we are called to a standard of holiness, not perfection. There is grace for you, right where you are. In motherhood and in life, the Lord's grace covers us and calls us to measure our lives according to the standard of Christ's righteousness. Being a Christ-follower means we walk by faith, demonstrating the fact that we are not perfect but are made holy because of God's unfailing love for us (Rom. 5:8).

We do not have to be perfect, even though there is a society-imposed pressure on moms to look and act the part. Instead, we have been set apart, and the beauty mark we should care about flaunting is not perfection, but God's love. Scripture tells us, "Above all, love each other deeply, because love covers over a multitude of sins" (1 Pet. 4:8). Rather than a standard of perfection, we are called to demonstrate a pattern of holiness. We are to put on the character traits of Christ in terms of faith, hope, love, compassion, gentleness, and grace.

Dirty dishes, mountains of stinky laundry, failed potty-training attempts and all, God's grace blankets our shortcomings. On days when you feel like a failure, remember that the race we are running is not of flesh and blood. It is not the physical that matters but what is inside of our hearts. Are we staying plugged into the source of God's truth and love? How are we leading and feeding our children? Are our hearts fixated and focused on Jesus? This is what matters in light of eternity. The Lord cares infinitely more about the conditions of our hearts than outward appearances.

When God sent Samuel to anoint the next king of Israel, He also said, "'The Lord does not look at the things people look at. People look at the outward appearance, but the Lord looks at the heart'" (1 Sam. 16:7). God called the shepherd David, whom he chose to be king, "a man after my own heart" (Acts 13:22). The Lord was unconcerned that David was short in stature, of humble occupation, and maybe not the strongest or most manly-looking of men. God chose David because of his heart of worship, his sold-out devotion to the Lord God.

The next time you fly out the door with no makeup on, leaving your dirty dishes, stinky laundry, and living room littered with toys behind, know that it matters not what you look like or what state your house is in but rather the conditions of your heart. Ask yourself, "How can I love my neighbor as myself? In what way can I bless another? Have I spoken about Jesus today? Have I spoken to Jesus today? How can I adopt a lifestyle of worship? Am I loving God with my heart, soul, mind, and strength?" These matters impact the eternal and reflect the internal conditions of our hearts.

Crucified with Christ

These are the words of Paul, spoken with passion, in defense of his faith: "I have been crucified with Christ and I no longer live, but Christ lives in me. The life I now live in the body, I live by faith in the Son of God, who loved me and gave himself for me. I do not set aside the grace of God, for if righteousness could be gained through the law, Christ died for nothing!" (Gal. 2:20-21). The message of the Gospel is deeply rooted in the fact that we are not perfect in and of ourselves. We all have a desperate need for Jesus.

Christ died to save us from having to live perfect lives to obtain eternal life with God in Heaven. In order to be known and fully loved by God for all of eternity, all we have to do is accept His grace. The blood of Jesus paved a way for us to get to Heaven. Jesus extends His hand to you with a present to offer. Cherish the free gift of salvation Christ wants to give you.

We have been called to live lives of love in honor of the great love God displayed for us in sending His only Son to die on a wooden cross. His pain was our eternal gain. We are to live changed lives because of what Jesus Christ did for us. As heirs of His grace, our sin has been crucified with Christ, and this is not of or from ourselves. We must depend on God's grace daily, realizing we are utterly lost without it. Choose grace over perfection. Only through God's saving grace in Christ Jesus can our lives be truly perfected.

Being perfected by Jesus, or made holy, is a process that occurs through osmosis. Osmosis is the process of molecules passing through a semipermeable membrane, equalizing the concentrations on either side. Although we will never be equal to Christ, we must strive to encompass the holy traits that Christ demonstrated on earth: indiscriminate love, faith in the unseen, hope for the future, sold-out devotion to the Lord God, selflessness, forgiveness, prayer, friendship, obedience, and compassion. We must surround and immerse our minds in the things of Christ, God's Word, and holy communion with His Spirit through prayer. We must assimilate our ways of thinking and behaving, adopting daily disciplines that establish godly character in order to know Jesus and grow into His likeness.

Dear Jesus,

Thank You for Your love and grace. I pray that You would help me to stop striving, to recognize and accept Your grace, and to live from the love

You relentlessly bestow upon me. Help me to lavish Your love on my husband, children, and all who I encounter in this lifetime. Show me ways that I can love and bless others today.

Thank You for Your grace, which covers my sins. Thank You for dying on the cross, so that I might live a life free from worldly standards. Help me to represent You well by loving others and caring more about the internal conditions of my heart rather than external appearances.

Thank You for being the perfect Sacrifice and for saving me from my sins and the consequence of eternal separation from You. Thank You that I get to be with You forever in Heaven someday. Thank You for the Holy Spirit and for Your perfect love.

In Jesus' flawless Name, amen.

Steps of Faith:

- Pinpoint one way that you can bless another person today. Live out your calling and walk in love. Even if it feels awkward, or seems uncomfortable, we are called to a standard of holiness. Reach out to someone, maybe through a kind text or a quick call. Ask the Lord to show you a specific way that you can bless another today.

- In a spiritual sense, if you were able to hold a mirror up to your heart and see what was inside, what would appear? Would the ripe fruits of the Spirit come to light; or would discord, dysfunction, and distress be evident? Pray to the Lord. Ask Him to take away anything that is hindering you from living a sold-out life for Christ Jesus.

14
Filled to the Brim

I pray that out of his glorious riches he may strengthen you with power through his Spirit in your inner being, so that Christ may dwell in your hearts through faith. And I pray that you, being rooted and established in love, may have power, together with all the Lord's holy people, to grasp how wide and long and high and deep is the love of Christ, and to know this love that surpasses knowledge— that you may be filled to the measure of all the fullness of God.

Ephesians 3:16-19

HAVE YOU EVER FELT COMPLETELY empty inside? There have been times that I have forgotten what my life looked like before becoming a mom. There have been moments of wishing that I could take back a piece of the freedom from my former life. There have been daily struggles of feeling like what I do is insignificant. I love my children—oh, so much. But my friends, motherhood is a sacrifice. It makes us holier and draws us closer to the heart of God. Sometimes, this refinement process is painful, like silver being purified through the fire.

On the contrary, there are days that my heart is filled to the brim and my soul hums a joyful song. I have noticed these are the days that I have typically delved into God's Word and have bowed my head to pray. These are the days that I have read to my children from their children's Bibles and have asked the Holy Spirit to intercede in their hearts. These are the days that my self-talk and thoughts gracefully land on the side of what is "true . . . noble . . . right . . . pure . . . lovely . . . admirable . . . excellent or praiseworthy" (Phil. 4:8). These are the days that the song of my heart sings the verses of Psalm 9:1-2: "I will give thanks to you, Lord, with all my heart; I will tell of all your wonderful deeds. I will be glad and rejoice in you; I will sing the praises of your name, O Most High."

I want this to be the song of my heart; therefore, my hands must follow the rhythm. As moms, it is imperative that we are reading God's Word. It is essential that we are imparting our children with the knowledge of the Gospel and inserting godly principles and the name of Jesus into their daily lives. It is salient that we believe the truth of the matter: motherhood matters! We must rise up and believe that our roles are irreplaceable and have the potential to impact eternities. We must do things and think thoughts that edify and fill our hearts to the brim each day so that our spirits sing and we can be lights in our children's lives.

Build A Boat

There is a Colton Dixon song on the radio called, "Build A Boat," that keeps playing on repeat in my head. The lyrics relay the message that, like Noah, we are to "build a boat" at various times in our lives when the Lord calls us to step out in faith. We are commanded to live by faith and build a boat even when we are in a dry, desert place.

It was sprinkling outside, and my windshield wipers acted as a metronome when this song came on for the second time while driving home from antique-shopping. It seemed as if God was tapping me on the shoulder, like a kind but firm teacher whispering, "Listen up!"

The song is a beautiful illustration of God's love and faithfulness. The lyrics build a bridge from the biblical story of Noah that spans across time and reaches over into our everyday lives, causing us to analyze our hearts and recommit ourselves to the plans of Jesus in our lives. Even if those plans entail building a boat in the desert where it never rains, we are called to pick up our hammers and to trust and believe in Jesus. God loved Noah so much that He commanded him to build a boat on dry land. God commands us to live for Him, to demonstrate His love, and to speak the name of Jesus, even when there is no recognition or monetary gain.

Recently, I was speaking with a writer friend of mine; and she reminded me of a big, simple truth that I had forgotten. She said something to the effect of, "It's not how many people buy my book or read my blog but the possibility of reaching even one person for Jesus that makes writing completely worth it." What simple, profound truth.

This principle is relevant in motherhood. Motherhood is a great sacrifice. But it is a sacrifice that is completely worth it. God sees us and cares about our faithfulness as moms, which makes all of our hard work, blood, sweat, and tears completely worthwhile. Our daily diligence and seemingly unnoticed effort matter to the Lord, and that is what truly matters. Through motherhood, we have the possibility of reaching our children for Jesus.

Our measure of being great moms should be based on our children's hearts and not outward achievements. Even so, our job is not to change our children's hearts but to encourage them toward Christ. In order to have an impact, we must be seeking Jesus for ourselves, cultivating the conditions of our hearts first and foremost.

Whatever it is in your life that brings glory to God, keep shining your light. When momentary circumstances and struggles blind you and all you can see is darkness all around, may your ulterior senses be reminded that darkness and light cannot coexist. People notice when you live, love, and speak the name of Jesus in your daily life. Be a lighthouse for Christ, an ever-present reminder of the safety and security Christ has to offer.

Even when it seems there is no one around who needs to be found, continue to shine. Have faith that they are out there, perhaps a little lost in a sea of darkness. Your glint of light might be all that they can spot from miles and miles away. That light is nothing but Christ in you. We are totally, completely, 100 percent lost without the saving grace of Jesus. He is the reason we have hope and light inside of us. Rely on His love and grace. Have grace for yourself and others.

Build a boat, even when it feels pointless, superfluous, and maybe even a little hopeless. Build. With Christ, there is hope. There is a reason behind God's assignments in our lives. Our job is to remain faithful in all that the Lord has called us to. Trust that God will provide the rain. Build a boat, even when you are in a dry, desert place.

Although we go unnoticed at times, that does not mean the God of the Universe does not recognize the outpouring of our love and care. God promises in His Word, "'So if you faithfully obey the commands I am giving you today—to love the Lord your God and to serve him with all your heart and with all your soul—then I will send rain on your land in its season, both autumn and spring rains, so that you may gather in your grain, new wine and olive oil'" (Deut. 11:13-14). I have a theory that God notices us even more as moms because motherhood is so often a thankless task. In the Bible, Jesus always had this special way of taking care of those the world deemed insignificant: the lepers, the blind, the lame, women, and children.

Motherhood demands that we set aside what we would like to do and trade it in for what needs to be done for our children. Being a mom is a selfless role, no doubt. That does not discount the difficulty it takes to lay down certain components of our lives in order for our children to live their best lives. Being a mother is an amazing role. Even so, the process of selfless sacrifice can be a painfully challenging one. I have found that the longer I am enlisted in this mom gig, the easier the sacrifices are to make. But when I was a brand-new mom, the transition from taking care of "me" to taking care of "we" was a difficult one.

Rest assured, you are not alone. You are seen, heard, and loved. In motherhood and in life, God notices your hard work and sacrifice. Your labors of love are precious in His sight. Mama, your heart is beautiful. You are holy, fully, and dearly loved by the Lord Jesus Christ.

From Empty to Encompassed in His love

On days when feelings of emptiness threaten to envelop me, I cling tightly to the truth of God's Word. Jesus has faced every emotion we have ever felt. He can relate to us and fill us with His love and Divine favor. When we are weak, Christ is our strength (2 Cor. 12:8-9).

Cry out to Jesus. Reveal to Him your heart and your hurt. The Lord wants to be your Strong Tower. Go to Jesus in prayer and empty out every emotion that you harbor. Let the Lord be your Lighthouse.

The book of Isaiah says about Jesus, "He was despised and rejected—a man of sorrows, acquainted with deepest grief . . . He was beaten so we could be whole. He was whipped so we could be healed" (Isa. 53:3-5). Jesus was beaten many times with a cat o' nine-tails before He was crucified. A crown of thorns was crushed onto His head. Spikes were driven through His hands and feet. Jesus endured so much pain. What was the purpose? So we could be healed, saved from our sins, forgiven, and set free. Allow the Lord's love and sacrifice to heal you of any hurt you harbor. Invite Him in to fully encompass the emptiness inside of you.

The thing about being empty inside is that there is room for something new and beautiful to begin to grow. The less there is of me, the more room there is for Christ's love to take root in my heart. Let God's love flourish and abide in you.

There is a void present inside of each and every one of us, but this cavity can be filled by the Creator of the world. Allow God's love to fill you. Do not turn to other things that will continue to cause you to come up short. Trade in that void for more of Jesus' presence in your daily life. Fill the God-shaped hole inside of your heart by reading the Bible and through prayer. Cultivate goodness in your soul by straining your innermost thoughts through the colander of who God says you are as "a chosen people, a royal priesthood, a holy nation, God's special possession, that you may declare the praises of him who called you out of darkness into his wonderful light" (1 Pet. 2:9). Allow the

Holy Spirit to grow up inside of you and produce ripe fruit that is tangible and edifying to others.

Share your fruit. We were not meant to "mom" alone. There are other moms out there who want to come alongside you in your motherhood journey. Believe it or not, other moms exist that want to meet you in the midst of your mess and become friends. Do not think your schedule has to be wiped clean, your house sparkling, or your to-do list mastered before you prioritize friendship. Let other ladies in. Reach out to some Christian mamas and allow the roots of friendship to establish and grow in your life. Your heart will be edified when you do.

> *Dear Jesus,*
>
> *Thank You that I am fully encompassed in Your love. When I feel empty inside, I pray that You would fill me with the knowledge of Your life-giving presence. Thank You for always being near. Thank You for the gift of motherhood. Thank You that I get to be a mom and become transformed through this holy sanctification process that You have designed and have specifically assigned for me.*
>
> *Rid me of myself. Help my heart to reflect more of You and less of me. Fill me to the brim with the joy of Your holy presence. Help me to reach out to other Christian women and develop deep-rooted friendships that are built on the foundation of Your great love. Help me to be on the lookout for other mamas who might need a friend today.*
>
> *In Jesus' wonderful Name, amen.*

Steps of Faith:

- Do something spiritually filling with your time today. Whether that is reading an online Bible study, choosing to listen to the Christian radio station, getting into God's Word, or praying for five minutes, choose to route your day with godly checkpoints.

- Reach out to an acquaintance and get her number. If you already have her number, schedule a time to get together. Either way, make a plan to engage with another Christian mama this week.
- Check out and listen to the podcast, "Don't Mom Alone," by Heather MacFadyen. It stresses the importance of not "momming" alone and discusses a plethora of different subjects relating to motherhood from a Christian point of view. (It is my favorite podcast!)

15
Chosen

"Therefore, as God's chosen people, holy and dearly loved, clothe yourselves with compassion, kindness, humility, gentleness and patience. Bear with each other and forgive one another if any of you has a grievance against someone. Forgive as the Lord forgave you. And over all these virtues put on love, which binds them all together in perfect unity."

Colossians 3:12-15

HAVE YOU EVER FELT LIKE you were not the best mom? I have! There have been many moments when I have wondered, *Why me, God? Why did You choose me to be these precious kiddos' mama?* I think my kids are extraordinary; so at times, I wonder why God chose ordinary, little me to mother such uniquely beautiful creations.

You are the mom for the job. God *chose* you, and it is time that you stop believing the lies of Satan that scream, "You aren't good enough" and instead start believing the truth of God's Word that says "you are a chosen people, a royal priesthood" (1 Pet. 2:9), dearly loved (John 3:16), created in advance for specifically assigned good works (John 15:16).

You have been hand-picked to be the mother of your children by the Creator of the universe. It is time that you "mom up" and start believing this truth about yourself. It is time that you mother your children in honor of the fact that you are the woman for the job. It is time that you start resting in God's grace and stop being harsh on yourself as God's chosen and dearly loved possession.

Carpe diem! Seize the day. You have been chosen in advance for good works, according to the Lord's will. Clothe yourself with God's righteousness through compassion, kindness, gentleness, humility, and patience. Live from the love of Christ, which declares you as the chosen mom for the task of raising your babies. It is no coincidence that you are the mother of your children. God has specifically selected you. Rise up! You are chosen. Live from this truth.

Some of the final words of Jesus recorded in the book of Matthew are, "'Therefore go and make disciples of all nations, baptizing them in the name of the Father and of the Son and of the Holy Spirit'" (Matt. 28:19). What did Jesus mean when He proclaimed this grand finale call to action? Are we meant to go overseas and preach the Word of Jesus? Perhaps! This is definitely not a bad idea. But, as moms, in this season that we are currently in, I know one thing is for certain: the disciple-making process starts in our homes. Our children need to hear the Word of God. Let us edify their hearts and minds each day through the powerful and effective words of Jesus found in the Bible.

Discipling can be very challenging to do when your kids are itty bitty. Invest in a children's Bible that resonates with your soul and read it to your children every day. Through daily diligence, you may come to find that the "children's" Bible opens your eyes to some valuable faith lessons along the way and draws you closer to God's heart.

Motivated Mama

Seeing through the lens of a child and having a childlike faith that wholly and fully trusts in the Lord is precious in His sight. We need to get back to that! We need to return to having faith on fire when it comes to knowing Jesus and spreading God's love. We need to live from the love of Jesus inside our hearts, unsurrendering. We need to dance each day in the light of Christ and reflect

God's glory. Jesus is "'the way and the truth and the life'" (John 14:6). Does your heart overflow with a resemblance and resonance of this truth?

The Gospel of Jesus Christ was meant to be shared. It was meant to spread. Like a forest fire caused by a tiny spark, the Gospel of Jesus is powerful, refining, and contagious. Teach your children the meaning of the song, "This Little Light of Mine," by the way you live your life.

We are creations of the King, reflections of the Lord Most High. As Christian mamas, we are called to rise up and be ambassadors for Christ. We were made to crave Jesus, created to live life undaunted and unashamed, proclaiming Jesus' name.

Disciple-making starts in our homes. Having a faith on fire should be something our children notice about our lives. The Bible should be out on our kitchen tables, being read to our children, edifying our hearts and theirs every single day. Is there grace in this regard? Yes! But our love for Jesus should motivate us to strive to get into the Word.

My high school cross country coach used to say, in regard to practicing on the weekends and over holidays, "Motivated people find ways." Some seasons of mom life make it incredibly challenging to consistently be in the Word. Jesus offers us His grace, but do not forget to be diligent and faithful. "Motivated people find ways." Be a motivated mama for Jesus.

Ann Voskamp once said, "I believe with every fiber of my being that when we live into a cruciform story with our children, the Holy Spirit never stops whispering to them and calling them home.4 We live within the tension of a Gospel story in raising our children. The push comes from giving unconditional love and grace; and the pull is catalyzed by imparting wisdom, correction, and discipline. We have been chosen to encompass all of these things. So long as we are connected to the source of God's truth, this same truth is siphoned into the hearts and lives of our children.

---

4   Heather MacFadyen, "Signpost Parenting: Ann Voskamp [ep. 394]," January 30, 2023 in *Don't Mom Alone*, podcast audio, 55:07, https://heathermacfadyen.com/2023/01/30/signpost-parenting-ann-voskamp-ep-395.

Do not give up. Do not lose heart. We have been chosen to impart Gospel truth and principles into our children's minds but not apart from Christ. We need the fire hydrant of God's wisdom, grace, and love. We need Christ's character as the source of our connection. We need faith, hope, and love running through our daily lives. We need our Bibles open and alive, acting as a hose of Christ's living water when our children's parched hearts need it most. We cannot be Jesus to our children; but we can direct them to the source of where His living water, love, and grace abound.

Dear Jesus,

Thank You for my children. Please help me to infuse their hearts with more of You. I pray that Your holy presence will watch over my home and edify my children's hearts each day. Use me as a vessel, Jesus, and teach me how to show my children Your love. Help them to be receptive to the truth at an early age. I pray that my faith would be a powerful example to my children. Help me to live boldly for You, Lord God.

Thank You for choosing me to be the mother of my children. They are such a blessing in my life. I know they will be a blessing in the lives of many others along the way. Lord, guide my children to the foot of Your cross. I pray that my children come to depend on You not only as their Savior, in times of need, but also as their Lord. I pray that they will delight in You and that You become their hope and treasure. I pray for these things over my life as well.

Give me strength, daily endurance, and wisdom as a mom. Cultivate the character traits of Christ's compassion, kindness, grace, and love within my heart.

In Jesus' faithful Name, amen.

Steps of Faith:

- If you do not own a children's Bible, purchase one. If you do, pull it out and place it somewhere common, within sight, where you will be reminded to read it to your children each day, starting today.

- Read 1 Peter 2:9 and John 15:16. These verses speak to our hearts about who we are as chosen daughters of the King.
    - "But you are a chosen people, a royal priesthood, a holy nation, God's special possession, that you may declare the praises of him who called you out of darkness into his wonderful light" (1 Pet. 2:9).
    - "'You did not choose me, but I chose you and appointed you so that you might go and bear fruit—fruit that will last—and so that whatever you ask in my name the Father will give you'" (John 15:16).
- Focus on one specific character trait of Christ that you want to cultivate within yourself today. Choose from the following: faith, compassion, kindness, gentleness, humility, patience, grace, and self-control. What is one practical way you can exude this trait?

Set Free

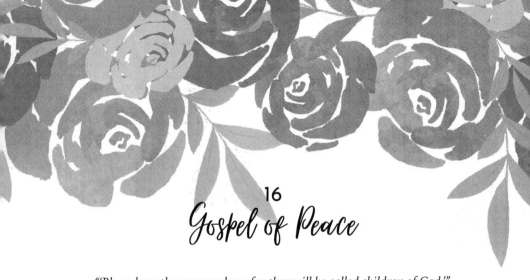

16
Gospel of Peace

"'Blessed are the peacemakers, for they will be called children of God.'"

Matthew 5:9

PEACE-FILLED PARENTS EQUAL HAPPY CHILDREN. While I am certain this is true, it is difficult to maintain peace in my heart and home at all times. Motherhood entails noisy toddlers, potty accidents on the carpet, and marker streaks on the walls. Being a mom consists of little-to-no makeup each day, lack of time for self, and limited free time, period. Motherhood often pushes my limits, tests my patience, and drags me outside of the boundaries of peace in my life. This is something that needs to be addressed because I cannot help but wonder, *Am I the only one?*

The answer to this question is a resounding, "No." I am not the only one who walks this road, who travels the tumultuous trails of motherhood. I am not the only one living day in and day out, in the mash of the daily grind, mommying littles. I am not the only mom out there confronted head-on with the giant of anxiety and stress in her life. I am not the only one who struggles with maintaining a mindset of peace in motherhood.

The Bible says, "Let the peace of Christ rule in your hearts, since as members of one body you were called to peace. And be thankful" (Col. 3:15). I do not know about you; but I often let the peace in my life get overruled by anxiety, worry, and fear. I get anxious over my to-do list. I worry about my children's health and safety. I fear when I cannot figure out all the logistics of how I am going to manage my children in the airport during an unexpected four-hour layover. I fear when I cannot find a desperately needed babysitter to go to a simple teeth cleaning or doctor's appointment. I get anxious when I feel like I can barely take care of myself, let alone my children. And yet, I can hear my Savior gently whisper in my heart, "'I am with you always'" (Matt. 28:20).

Fear is not of or from the Lord, and that is why we need to learn how to trade in our fearful thoughts with the peace of Christ. Philippians 4:6-8 says, "Do not be anxious about anything, but in every situation, by prayer and petition, with thanksgiving, present your requests to God. And the peace of God, which transcends all understanding, will guard your hearts and your minds in Christ Jesus." The author of Philippians, the apostle Paul, goes on to say, "Finally, brothers and sisters, whatever is true, whatever is noble, whatever is right, whatever is pure, whatever is lovely, whatever is admirable—if anything is excellent or praiseworthy—think about such things." Might I add that Paul wrote these divine words while in a jail cell! These words are the lyrics of the song of peace written upon my heart. It is what I cling to when my world around me starts to spin. On days that feel out of control, I refuse to give into the twister and instead let God's Word do its holy work inside of me, reminding me of the solid Rock of my foundation, Jesus Christ.

Free time is a scarcity in my daily life. This makes the number-one thing on my to-do list—getting into God's Word—a challenge. Our precious free time is so limited because having little ones requires all of us for what seems like all of the time. I long to be in God's Word more often; but when potty training a two-year old, free time becomes a famine. After my kids go down for naps, it is "go time" for me to dive into God's Word. I encourage you to carve out time in your day to read God's precious book of truth. It will give you peace and "guard your hearts and minds in Christ Jesus" (Phil. 4:7).

Peace can overflow from the wellsprings of our hearts when it is bubbling up inside of us. In the Bible, we are called to "guard [our] heart" "above all else" (Prov. 4:23). Surrounding our lives with Scripture and prayer is such an asset because, as moms, we are under spiritual attack. The enemy would like nothing more than for us to lose our focus in living for God, lose our footing in discipling our children, and fumble before getting into the Word. But Paul describes peace as part of the armor of God that enables us to resist Satan's schemes (Eph. 6:13-15).

We need to band together as mothers in Christ and choose the peace of Christ's holy presence to reign in our lives. It is a mindful choice that has to be made every day—sometimes hourly, sometimes by the minute. If we can take cognizant steps of faith toward the cross in the direction of Christ's peace through reading the Bible, writing Scripture on our hearts, and spending time in prayer, we will stand ready and be equipped, wearing the full armor of God, activated through Christ Jesus.

Dear Jesus,

Equip me with the Gospel of peace. Write Your Word upon my heart so that I can stand ready with my feet outfitted in your shoes of peace, ready to walk in the direction of the cross, away from fear, anxiety, and all else that wages war against Your peace present in my life.

Thank You for Your Holy Spirit, that I have direct access to the source of Your peace and power. I pray that Your holy presence would calm my anxious heart and surpass the whirlwind of my worried thoughts throughout the day.

Jesus, I trade in my fear for Your peace through the power of the Holy Spirit. Equip me today with Your battle armor through God's Word and prayer. Protect me against the schemes of the enemy. Robe me in Your peace and love.

In Jesus' mighty Name, amen.

Steps of Faith:

- Write God's Word upon your heart. Start by taking some time to read Psalm 23. Write a summary of what this psalm means to you.

- When the worries of your mind start to swirl and the tempest of anxiety threatens your stability, choose faith over fear. Lace up your sandals of peace that come from the Gospel—God's Word—and the hope we have in Jesus Christ. Stand firm on God's promises (Eph. 6:14-15). Jot down a verse that reminds you of the steadfastness of God's peaceful presence in your life. Place the verse somewhere within sight in your home. If nothing specific comes to mind, record John 16:33 as a daily reminder that our peace comes from the Gospel and from our Savior, Jesus Christ: "'I have told you these things, so that in me you may have peace. In this world you will have trouble. But take heart! I have overcome the world'" Rest in Jesus' promise and put on the full armor of God!

17
The Pursuit of Holiness

"You were taught, with regard to your former way of life, to put off your old self, which is being corrupted by its deceitful desires; to be made new in the attitude of your minds; and to put on the new self, created to be like God in true righteousness and holiness."

Ephesians 4:22-24

I LOVE WATCHING MY CHILDREN play. It is one of my all-time favorite pastimes. I have a baby and two precious, sweet little ones, a boy and a girl, who love life, Mama, Dada, and their "lovies." I love my children beyond what I can fully describe. From the moment they were laid upon my chest in the hospital after giving birth, I was head over heels, totally, deeply in love. When I think about how much I love my children, I cannot help but think about how much God loves me. The love of a mother pales in comparison to the great love that Jesus has for us. Still, I love the analogy of a mother's love being like that of my Heavenly Father's. It is something tangible to which I can relate.

The love of Jesus far surpasses any knowledge or earthly understanding we have of life, love, and the pursuit of happiness in our lives. "The pursuit of happiness" should exist as "the pursuit of holiness" in the minds and hearts of Christ-followers. We are to live holy lives for Jesus and strive to stay away from acts of sin. We must live in the light through prayer, God's Word, and fellowship with other believers. In living holy lives, we set an example of godliness for our children.

Can happiness and holiness go hand in hand? Absolutely, 100 percent they can. But the fruit of happiness grows as a byproduct of a healthy holiness tree. Still, this fruit is not guaranteed, and we must continue to faithfully tend to our gardens of holiness—fruit or none—because we fear the Lord and want to honor Jesus. Ephesians 5:8-9 describes us this way: "For you were once darkness, but now you are light in the Lord. Live as children of light (for the fruit of the light consists in all goodness, righteousness and truth)."

God loves us despite our sin and disobedience. Does God care that we strive to walk obediently, in accordance with His Word and will? Absolutely, yes! But even when we fall short, God still loves us. Jesus offers us His love, grace, forgiveness, and freedom in full. Sin and all, Jesus loves us. For those of us in Christ, nothing can separate us from the love of God (Rom. 8:38-39).

Ask the Lord to bring to light anything that is hindering you from living a sold-out life of obedience for Christ. Repent, walk in a new light, and experience the fresh air of redemption. Ask the Holy Spirit to surround you on all sides of your life.

God's forgiveness is freeing. Like a beautiful forest hike, the sound of a baby's laughter, or a brilliant rainbow in the sky, God's forgiveness releases inhibition. It unfolds a newfound glory that allows us to live fully and experience the rapture of pure joy that stems from God's presence flowing freely in our daily lives. As Paul reminds us, "Where the Spirit of the Lord is, there is freedom" (2 Cor. 3:17). And where there is freedom, there is victory.

Allow God's Word to refine your life. Dwell on the Scriptures. Live with the fruits of the Spirit—"love, joy, peace, forbearance, kindness, goodness, faithfulness, gentleness, and self-control" (Gal. 5:22-23)—overflowing out of your life. Allow these fruits to ripen and grow. Give God the authority to prune you so that the fruit the Holy Spirit produces in your life will be edifying and bless the lives of others.

Live a sold-out life of surrender for Jesus each day. He loves you. He roots for you. He has paved a way for you through His consecrated blood. He wants you to walk in obedience in return out of love. Live a life free from sin and darkness. Walk in the light of salvation, God's love, and Christ's forgiveness each new day.

Unveiled Hearts

Moses' face would be filled with the radiance of the Lord after his encounters with God on Mount Sanai. His face would literally glow. This frightened people, naturally; and so he would veil his face to keep the Israelites from beholding the glory of the Lord as it shone through his countenance. Second Corinthians talks about a new law and order—the perfect law of Jesus Christ. Paul writes, "But whenever anyone turns to the Lord, the veil is taken away. Now the Lord is the Spirit, and where the Spirit of the Lord is, there is freedom. And we all, who with unveiled faces contemplate the Lord's glory, are being transformed into his image with ever-increasing glory, which comes from the Lord, who is the Spirit" (2 Cor. 3:16-18). Our faces are unveiled when we experience the Spirit of the Living God within us.

Jesus came to fulfill the Law given to Moses. Although the Ten Commandments are still applicable in our lives today, Jesus came as a form of living grace, so that we could experience forgiveness and freedom from our sins.

Another Old Testament "veil" could be found in the temple, the separation between the place of worship and the Holiest of Holies, where God's Spirit dwelled. In both cases, the veil has been torn because of Jesus' death and resurrection. Jews and Gentiles alike can come to know Jesus and behold His glory through salvation.

In a wedding, the bride's veil signifies purity and is a representation of modesty. When the wedding vows have been exchanged, the groom lifts the veil to see his bride's face after she says, "I do." The groom then beholds his wife's beauty with loving adoration. We are the bride of Christ. Jesus wants to remove the veil of our hearts so that our inner beauty can shine. In the same way a bride typically takes on her groom's last name, we, too, are a representation of Jesus Christ as "Christians." We have taken His name. In the same way we want to respect and honor our husbands, we should strive to honor, love, and live for the Lord in reverence of the cross.

We can live our lives with hearts unveiled through purifying ourselves of unwanted sin. Through repentance and God's forgiveness, we are made brand new. Do not live life with a veiled heart covered by sin and darkness. Ask Jesus to unveil you so that you can shine the radiance of His glory.

The writer of Hebrews unpacks for us the idea of the lifted veil in this way:

> Therefore, brothers and sisters, since we have confidence to enter the Most Holy Place by the blood of Jesus, by a new and living way opened for us through the curtain, that is, his body, and since we have a great priest over the house of God, let us draw near to God with a sincere heart and with the full assurance that faith brings, having our hearts sprinkled to cleanse us from a guilty conscience and having our bodies washed with pure water. Let us hold unswervingly to the hope we profess, for he who promised is faithful (Heb. 10:19-23).

Jesus was the veil. When His flesh was torn, we were released from a life of certain sin and bondage. Through the acceptance of Jesus in our hearts, the veil is lifted; and we are called to a new life in Christ Jesus. This new life consecrates our hearts and purifies our lives. We are called to a standard of holiness because Jesus Christ came and tore the veil.

The resurrected King has resurrected our hearts and lives. His ultimate sacrifice ushers hope and new life into our hearts. This new life is freedom from our sin. Freedom is a sanctification process that requires us to first, get free and second, stay free. We get free by asking for God's forgiveness with a sincerely repentant heart. We stay free through immersing ourselves in God's truth, and through prayer. We stay out of bondage through accountability, confession, and asking other people for their prayers. Do not hide and let your sin fester and grow in darkness. Unveil your sin and ask Jesus to step in. Through prayer, God's Word, and Christian accountability or counseling, we can live life with hearts unveiled.

> *Dear Jesus,*
>
> *Thank You for Your death and resurrection. Thank You that by Your stripes I am forgiven and set free from eternal bondage to sin. Thank You for dying on the cross so I might live a free life and have an eternal connection with You. Thank You for rolling the stone away from the tomb and removing the barrier between me and You for all eternity. Thank You for Your great love. Thank You, Jesus, for saving me.*
>
> *I pray that I will walk in obedience to Your Word and will. Reveal any hidden sin in my life that needs to be brought to light. Forgive me and make me new. I love You, Lord Jesus.*
>
> *In Jesus' holy Name, amen.*

Steps of Faith:

- Meditate on the words of this proverb: "Whoever conceals their sins does not prosper, but the one who confesses and renounces them finds mercy" (Prov. 28:13). Ask God to reveal to you any hidden sin or anything concealed in your life that is hindering you from living a sold-out life for Christ. Seek accountability. Repent and walk in a new light of redemption and freedom found in Jesus. Allow nothing to entangle or disqualify you from running this race for Christ with all your might!
- What do you need to be uprooted from within yourself in order for something of a godly nature to resurrect and grow in your

life? Is it a lack of patience, discontentment, jealousy, or an overly packed schedule? What specific changes do you need to make? Prayerfully give those things to the Lord and ask that He would enable something more beautiful to grow. Ask for God's love, patience, forgiveness, thankfulness, generosity, and self-control to flourish in you.

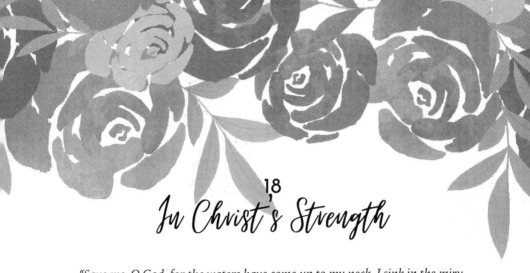

18
In Christ's Strength

"Save me, O God, for the waters have come up to my neck. I sink in the miry depths, where there is no foothold. I have come into the deep waters; the floods engulf me. I am worn out calling for help; my throat is parched."

Psalm 69:1-3

THE PSALMIST DAVID WROTE THESE words at a moment in time when he felt like he was in over his head, drowning in a sea of defeat. As moms, it is easy to feel this way when situations do not pan out according to plan or when extra helpings are added to our plates. But Psalm 69 goes on to assure us that we do not have to feel stuck in feeling overwhelmed or defeated: "But I pray to you, LORD, in the time of your favor; in your great love, O God, answer me with your sure salvation" (Ps. 69:13).

Psalm 69:13 shows us that we can use prayer to combat our feelings of being overwhelmed. Furthermore, Psalm 69:30-33 demonstrates how we can be triumphant through delighting in the Lord as our Strength. By having a mindset of worship and a spirit of thanksgiving, we can actually override our feelings of inadequacy. The Lord is our Help when we seek Him through prayer. The Lord hears our hearts and helps us to claim freedom in our lives through the Holy Spirit in Jesus' name.

David finishes Psalm 69 with a song of praise to the Lord: "I will praise God's name in song and glorify him with thanksgiving. This will please the Lord more than an ox, more than a bull with its horns and hooves. The poor will see and be glad—you who seek God, may your hearts live! The Lord hears the needy and does not despise his captive people" (Ps. 69:30-33).

Being a mom is like treading water for an extended period of time. Then you have your second child. While still treading water, you have just been handed a baby! Being a mom is not an easy feat. This is no secret. But what is the purpose behind the struggle?

I have heard it said, "You cannot pour from an empty cup." As a mother, I beg to differ. This is what we are called to do every day. Christ Divinely meets us in the middle of our struggles and is our Strength. Having an empty cup is the perfect opportunity for Christ to be able to step in and provide His miraculous portion for our every need.

We are called to be faithful. In matters big and matters small, we must rise to the occasion of our calling and be joyful creations as mothers who live life with Christ in the driver's seat of our lives. We must mother our children with the heart of God in mind. We must have God's Word written upon our hearts.

Keep running your race with all of your might. All of the pain, the toil, and the trials you face as a mom are not in vain. Use them to proclaim His name. Lean in and depend upon Christ like never before. He is the only One able to fill our empty hearts and make us feel complete. He is the Giver of promising peace and lasting joy.

I believe that the purpose of the struggles we face as moms is the Holy Spirit's way of prompting us to fully rely on Christ as our Strength, Support, and Daily Bread. There will be highs and lows in motherhood and in life. The secret is learning to lean in on Christ through it all. The purpose of motherhood is to sanctify our hearts, to renew our minds, and to transform our entire selves to be more like Christ Jesus.

Christ's Faithfulness Never Fails

The prophet Isaiah describes Jesus, the Messiah, in this way in Isaiah 42:3-4: "A bruised reed he will not break, and a smoldering wick he will not snuff out. In faithfulness he will bring forth justice; he will not falter or be discouraged till he establishes justice on earth. In his teaching the islands will put their hope" (Isa. 42:3-4). The loose definition of "a bruised reed" is a stalk of grain that is broken in such a way that it will never again produce. Becoming a mom changed me. I do not know quite how to describe it; but after my daughter was born, something inside me shifted. The "me" to "we" factor altered my entire mindset and redirected my thinking. Like an extra weight being added, motherhood put a little person in mind, calling out my name at the back of my mind all of the time.

If I am being completely honest, I did not like it at first. I loved my daughter dearly, but the extra weight felt heavy. When I finally realized my desperate need for Jesus to step in, I was able to take my burdensome feelings to the Lord. He yoked me to His peace and transformed my feelings of sorrow into gratitude, which led to joy. It was not an overnight fix, and the Lord is still refining me. But by depending on Jesus as my Daily Bread through God's Word, prayer, and counting my blessings, Jesus changed me.

Maybe you can relate. Maybe it is not motherhood but something else that is weighing you down. When we are discouraged, Christ's courage never falters. When we lose our way, the Lord knows exactly where we are and lovingly guides us back onto the road He has for us. When we lack faith, Christ's faithfulness never fails.

This is the good news: Christ goes before us. In motherhood and in life, He is our Portion when we have nothing left to give. He is our Strength when we feel weak and incapable. Christ's grace carries us when the motherhood road gets rough. (And it is going to get rough at times.) Christ never guaranteed this life would be easy. In fact, He said quite the opposite.

"In this world you will have trouble," but the good news is that Christ has "overcome this world" (John 16:33).

Dear Jesus,

Thank You for going before me in motherhood and in life. You provide a way, and Your ways are good. I praise You because You are forever faithful, without fail. I want to honor You with my life. May my heart, mind, and actions bring You glory.

Thank You for the gift of motherhood. Thank You for its refining properties and for using motherhood as a tool to draw me closer to Your heart. I love You, Lord. Thank You for Your goodness.

In Jesus' faithful Name, amen.

Steps of Faith:

- Read through Psalm 69:13-18. Read it a second time and highlight or underline the verse that stands out to you the most and use it as a means of support and encouragement today.
- Thank God for being your Strength and Portion. Call upon Him throughout the day and ask Him to provide for and meet your heart's needs.

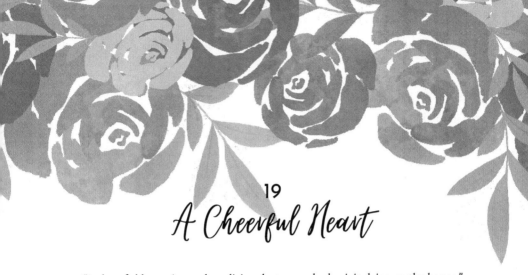

19
A Cheerful Heart

"A cheerful heart is good medicine, but a crushed spirit dries up the bones."

Proverbs 17:22

I LOVE THIS VERSE! ITS reference is written on a notecard, placed upon my desk. Every time that I review it, my heart is uplifted. A cheerful heart is one of the greatest gifts we can give our families.

In three words, how would you describe yourself? Does the word "positive" or a synonym of this adjective come to mind? The Bible says that we are to have cheerful hearts. This plays out in our daily lives as positivity. Positivity is powerful. Positivity is biblical. Positivity is what we are called to as mothers and Christ-followers.

How often do you smile? Smiling stimulates our minds and sets a tone of thanksgiving in our hearts. When we smile, it is hard to think negative thoughts. Smiling also influences the attitudes of those around you. It has the ability to sway hearts. Like a light switch, smiling gives us the capability of turning on a mindset of gratitude and joy. Smiling leads us to green pastures and quiet streams. Smiling enables us to dwell on what is "true . . . noble . . . right . . . pure . . . lovely . . . excellent or praiseworthy" (Phil. 4:8). Smile more often, Mama.

Be grateful. Instead of thinking of all that is wrong in your life and the lives of others, take the plank out of your own eye and adopt a heart and mentality of thankfulness. The Bible commands us to be thankful in all circumstances (1 Thess. 5:18).

Be joyful. Joy is a fruit of the Spirit. It is mentioned in the Bible many times as a positive trait we are to have and exude as followers of Jesus. In the English Standard Version of the Bible, "joy" or "joyful" is mentioned approximately 430 times. "Happiness" is only mentioned a total of ten times. Joy is a much stronger, longer lasting dose of happiness that relates to our hope in Christ and eternal life.

Joy is happiness deeply rooted in God's goodness. Nehemiah 8:10 says, "The joy of the Lord is your strength." Joy makes us strong in a spiritual sense. Joy tethers us to the heart of God and encapsulates our lives with God's goodness. The Bible calls us to "rejoice always" (1 Thess. 5:16). Let us have joyful hearts of thanksgiving that reflect the Lord's light. Let us be positive creations as mothers, wives, and followers of Christ. Let us put on the cap of thankfulness and joy, each new day.

The apostle Paul writes challenging words for us: "Rejoice always, pray continually, give thanks in all circumstances; for this is God's will for you in Christ Jesus" (1 Thess. 5:16-18). As a mom, it is all too easy to slip into my everyday routine with a lackluster attitude and forget to pray. At times, I fail to cultivate a heart and mindset of thanksgiving and resort to mentally whining and complaining. It is sad but true. I fail each day in so many ways; but through Christ, there is a better way, one that is hope-filled and full of joy.

With the Holy Spirit of Christ in me, I no longer have to live out my days in shame, fear, or defeat. I can authentically "rejoice always" because my salvation in Christ secures my eternity. My forever in Heaven with Jesus is a sealed deal. I can "pray continuously" and trust in the Holy Spirit to intercede and relay my needs and heart desires to His Holy Majesty. I can continue to seek Christ throughout the day, weighing my actions and motives against God's Word. I can live with the freedom power of "thanksgiving" pumping through my veins and coursing my path unto His Divine ways, plans, and purposes for me. And His purposes are good plans that give me radiant hope and a brilliant, perfectly pieced future (Jer. 29:11).

Not all moments in motherhood or life are happy ones; but as Christians, we are to exude His light. The word "Christian" derives from two Greek words: "Christ" and "tian." The Greek word *Christ* means "anointed one." *Tian* means "little." So the word "Christian" literally means "little anointed ones" or, in other words, "mini-Christs."[5] Like a stained-glass window, we have been purposed to reflect and refract Christ's light in unique and beautiful ways.

> *Dear Jesus,*
>
> *Thank You for Your joy present and overflowing in my life. Let me be a light and an example of what it is to be a positive, life-loving creation as a mom and wife. Although my true hope and joy await me in eternity, help me to live for You today in being joyful and positive. Help me to adopt a heart of thanksgiving, counting my blessings and realizing all that You have done and continue to do in my life.*
>
> *Thank You for Your presence. Thank You for Your hope that tangibly unfolds in my heart as I read God's Word. Thank You for Your truths and promises. Help me to adopt a heart of positivity and gladness today.*
>
> *In Jesus' beautiful Name, amen.*

Steps of Faith:

- Make a list of five things you are grateful for in your life today. Use that note as a bookmark or place it somewhere accessible as a beautiful reminder.
- Smile! Make a conscious effort to smile more often.
- Read and take some time to meditate on the Amplified Bible Version of 1 Thessalonians 5:16-19: "Rejoice always *and* delight

---

5   Jonathan K. Mickleson, "Christianos (a Christian) Χριστιανός, מְשִׁיחִי, Unabridged Version," last modified May 1, 2020. greek4christians.com/@Vocabulary_Topics/ Special_Vocabulary~Christianos%2C_Unabridged_version.

in your faith; be unceasing *and* persistent in prayer; in every situation [no matter what the circumstances] be thankful *and* continually give thanks *to God*; for this is the will of God for you in Christ Jesus. Do not quench [subdue, or be unresponsive to the working and guidance of] the [Holy] Spirit."

20
Using Scripture to Combat the lies

"The devil said to him, 'If you are the Son of God, tell this stone to become
bread.' Jesus answered, 'It is written: "Man shall not live on bread alone."'

Luke 4:3-4

WHEN JESUS WAS IN THE wilderness being tested by Satan, He endured forty days of clinging tightly to His faith. This is what we are called to as mothers and daughters of Christ. We must rely on the Scriptures that are written upon our hearts to fortify our minds in believing the truth of God's Word over the lies of the enemy.

Before the trials and temptations took place in the wilderness, Jesus was baptized by John the Baptist. He was equipped with the Holy Spirit directly prior to being tempted for forty days. God equips us for the trials and temptations we face each day as moms. When we are tempted to believe the lies of the devil, we must rehearse God's Word in our minds, breathe God's truth into our lives, and combat the lies with Scripture.

The enemy came at Jesus from different angles. Satan is tricky like that. He will pursue any and all means to get us to stumble, sin, and, in a way, worship him when we fall prey to his plans. We must dwell in God's Word each day and memorize portions of our Bibles so that we have a sword to use when the enemy comes our way.

Some of the lies we believe as moms are about ourselves; others are about our circumstances. Some of the lies pertain to our self-esteem: *I am not good enough; I will never measure up.* Other lies are directed at our spiritual walk with God and are aimed at our faith: *I am not godly enough.* All of the lies are meant to distract us from fulfilling the fullness of God's plans. Things like worry, doubt, and insecurity can be major roadblocks in our way of furthering the Kingdom of Heaven. The good news is that each and every flaming arrow Satan sends soaring our way can be snuffed out midair by means of the powerful and defensive Word of God.

Use the following Scriptures to combat the enemy and speak God's Truth over your life. Write these Scriptures on your heart and use them as your strength and shield:

- To lies about our self-esteem, the Lord says we are beautifully made: "I praise you because I am fearfully and wonderfully made; your works are wonderful, I know that full well" (Ps. 139:14).
- To lies that we will never measure up, God's Word says, "'My grace is sufficient for you, for my power is made perfect in weakness.' Therefore I will boast all the more gladly about my weaknesses, so that Christ's power may rest on me" (2 Cor. 12:9).
- To lies that we are nothing special, God says, "But you are a chosen people, a royal priesthood, a holy nation, God's special possession, that you may declare the praises of him who called you out of darkness into his wonderful light" (1 Pet. 2:9).
- To lies that we are not godly enough, God reminds us, "For it is by grace you have been saved, through faith—and this is not from yourselves, it is the gift of God—not by works, so that no one can boast" (Eph. 2:8-9).
- To our worry, the Lord whispers, "Do not be anxious about anything, but in every situation, by prayer and petition, with

thanksgiving, present your requests to God. And the peace of God, which transcends all understanding, will guard your hearts and your minds in Christ Jesus" (Phil. 4:6-7). And "You will keep in perfect peace all who trust in you, all whose thoughts are fixed on you!" (Isa. 26:3, NLT)

- To our doubt, God promises, "'For I know the plans I have for you,' declares the Lord, 'plans to prosper you and not to harm you, plans to give you hope and a future'" (Jer. 29:11).
- To our insecurity, Scripture declares, "The Lord is my rock, my fortress and my deliverer; my God is my rock, in whom I take refuge, my shield and the horn of my salvation, my stronghold" (Ps. 18:2).

Because Jesus is the perfect Example of how we are to live our lives, we must do as Christ did in the wilderness when under spiritual attack. We must strive to prepare against the schemes of the enemy through immersing our hearts and minds in God's Word. We need the Bible as our sword and faith in God's promises as our shield. Pray that the Lord would surround you on all sides of your life, and bring the truth of His promises to light when darkness creeps in.

Dear Jesus,

Help me to rely on You when I am tested and tried. I lean into You and Your Word to uplift me and be my Guiding Light. Thank You for the truth of Your Word. Thank You that You are a faithful God and that Your promises withstand the test of time. Your Word is alive and applicable to my life today, tomorrow, and forever. Thank You for the timeless message and example we have of the Lord Jesus Christ to show us the way. Thank You for providing us an escape route through Your Word when under spiritual attack.

In Jesus' mighty Name, amen.

Steps of Faith:

- Read 1 Corinthians 10:13: "No temptation has overtaken you except what is common to mankind. And God is faithful; he will not let you be tempted beyond what you can bear. But when you are tempted, he will also provide a way out so that you can endure it." Remember that God always provides a way out when we undergo trials and temptations in life. Oftentimes, the way out is through God's Word. Pray and seek the Lord through His Word when faced with something that seems like more than you can handle.

- Record whatever lie you have been struggling with lately on a piece of toilet paper using a marker. Flush that piece of paper down the toilet and say a prayer asking God to release you from its grip and to equip you to fight back against the lie with Scripture in Jesus' powerful Name.

Mom Life

21
Three 3 and Under!

"Jesus answered, 'Everyone who drinks this water will be thirsty again, but whoever drinks the water I give them will never thirst. Indeed, the water I give them will become in them a spring of water welling up to eternal life.'"

John 4:13-14

HAVING THREE SMALL CHILDREN THREE years of age and under is a mountain-moving task. Is it rewarding? Yes! Are there joyful moments that are laced with God's grace and transparent cracks exuding glimpses of Heaven? Absolutely! But some days are just plain difficult.

In the rough patches of whining, crying, temper tantrums, picky-eating habits, and potty-training accidents, I feel my blood start to boil and my heart rate elevate to match its fight-or-flight state of adrenaline. In these difficult moments, on the tough days, I have found that the more prep work I have already done to immerse myself in God's grace, the better able and equipped I am to draw from the well of God's grace and offer my children a drink. When I am getting in the Word, practicing the discipline of reading the Bible, and entering into His courts through prayer, I am better able to offer my children the precious gift of God's goodness overflowing from the wellsprings of my heart. I am a more graceful, God-filled mother on days when I am able to connect with the heart of God.

There is much intrinsic value to be found in a woman who is daily connected to the cross of Christ. There is beauty to behold in a lost woman who is able to truly be found in coming humbly before God, entering into His holy presence each day. We catch glimpses of Heaven when the people we know and love live from the source of His great love. What greater gift could I offer my family than Jesus alive in me?

The book of Proverbs gives a picture of what this woman who walks with God looks like: "Her children arise and call her blessed; her husband also, and he praises her: 'Many women do noble things, but you surpass them all.' Charm is deceptive, and beauty is fleeting; but a woman who fears the Lord is to be praised" (Prov. 31:28-30). On days when I find myself feeling snappy and rushed, I must pump the brakes and reflect on God's goodness by giving Him thanks and becoming more in tune and alert to the Holy Spirit in my life through prayer. Being daily steeped in God's grace is so important to us as Christian mamas. When we accept the drink Jesus offers us at the well, we are more likely to extend it to our children and to others who are desperate for the source of God's love, grace, and eternal life through Jesus Christ our Lord and Savior.

"Quiet" Time

"I just don't have the time." How often do we say or think these words? For me, it happens quite often. I have learned my limits and how to say "no" when necessary. In the words of Lysa TerKeurst, "A Best Yes will require having the courage to say no to other things. No to wrong things. No to seemingly good things. That's the only way to ensure there's space to run and take that leap of faith toward the best things."[6] One thing I *do* need more of in my life is God. As a mother of three small children, this can present itself as a challenging task. I have to intentionally take the time to connect with the heart of God each day through His Word and prayer.

---

6   Lysa TerKeurst, *The Best Yes* (Nashville: Thomas Nelson, 2014), 62.

As a mom with my hands full, this does not always come to fruition in the form of a full-blown, lengthy quiet time. Quite the opposite. My "quiet times" are usually laced with my children's laughter, chasing, and make-believe play. In such a good way, my "quiet times" are graced by my children's presence. I consider myself blessed.

I have found that it is okay to put in my earbuds and open up my Bible (or Bible app) for five minutes and pray that the Lord would bless my time spent in His presence. The Holy Spirit is fully able to multiply my offering and fill up my heart with Jesus' Divine portions. I humbly offer Him what I have—which is sometimes only five or ten minutes, with business in the background—and trust that like the few loaves of bread and fish the boy had to offer, Jesus can multiply my meager portions because He sees my heart and is moved by my desire to know Him more.

Mark 8:2 says, "Jesus called his disciples to him and said, 'I have compassion for these people; they have already been with me three days and have nothing to eat.'" He Himself then miraculously met their need by multiplying the loaves and fishes present to feed four thousand people. In the same way, Jesus has compassion on us when we are hungry to know Him more fully, to follow His footsteps more fearfully, to love God and others more fiercely, and to faithfully rely on His miraculous provision in our daily lives. He reminds us, "'But seek first his kingdom and his righteousness, and all these things will be given to you as well'" (Matt. 6:33).

Dear Jesus,

Thank You for time spent in Your Word and prayer. No matter how little or how much, I pray that I would be able to offer You my heart and presence in full each day. Please multiply and bless my time spent with You. Fill my heart through Your Word and prayer. Help me to be faithful in knowing, loving, and living for You more fully through the knowledge and

understanding of the Bible. Open my heart to be able to understand Your
Word and walk in Your ways.

In Jesus' precious Name, amen.

Steps of Faith:

- Say a short prayer praising and thanking God for His love and faithfulness in your life.
- Download the "First 5" app by Proverbs 31 Ministries. This app has a daily portion of Scripture that is accompanied by an article written by a Christian author who is theologically and spiritually based, followed by a prayer. Choose to get into God's Word each day, using this app, before scrolling.
- Read Luke 16:10: "Whoever can be trusted with very little can also be trusted with much, and whoever is dishonest with very little will also be dishonest with much." Consider this verse in light of what it means to be a mom and be faithful in raising children, to the best of your ability, according to godly precepts and biblical standards.

22
A Strong Offense

"Remember this: Whoever sows sparingly will also reap sparingly,
and whoever sows generously will also reap generously."

2 Corinthians 9:6

WHEN I WAS A GIRL, my soccer coach told our team, "The team who shoots the most wins." He did not say the team that scores the most wins. He stressed the fact that the team that takes the most shots will win the game. Whether this is true 100 percent of the time in the game of soccer, I am unsure. But what I do know is that we are to take the most shots we can at our children's hearts.

Throughout each day, opportunities arise for us to shoot. Shoot to score. Tell them about Jesus. Practice godly discipline. Be kind and loving. Let your words be full of grace. Demonstrate the fruits of the Spirit. When opportunities arise for you to coach, do so with all of your might. Speak the name of Jesus into your children's lives. Know that you will not score a goal with every shot. But take as many shots as you possibly can. "The team who shoots the most wins."

As a mom, take shots to win over your children's hearts for Jesus. As God commanded the people of Israel, "'These commandments that I give you today are to be on your hearts. Impress them on your children. Talk about them when you sit at home and when you walk along the road, when you lie down and when you get up'" (Deut. 6:6-7).

Not only should we take a defensive stance but also an offensive position in what we say for our children's ears to hear and hearts to absorb. Mommy and Daddy are their greatest influences and role models. It is our God-given role to pray with our children and impart them with words of biblical wisdom, truth, salt, and light each day. We do this through prayer. We do this by weaving the message of the Gospel throughout their daily lives. Teach your children the meaning of grace through their own shortcomings. When an opportunity arises, impart your children with the message of Jesus.

Explain to your children the message of Jesus' love through the miracles that He performed and what He did for us on the cross. Read them Old Testament stories from God's Word that highlight the power and "bigness" of God. But also, show them Jesus' love, grace, and greatness when opportunities arise. Show them and explain. When modern-day miracles happen, verbally acknowledge the greatness and goodness of our mighty God. Create a bridge from biblical times that spans across centuries and connects to our lives today.

In the loud culture we live in, we must be super intentional. The world is not shy about teaching our children ungodly precepts and language. We must develop a strong offense in our children's lives and impart them with God's teachings to an even greater degree. It is a spiritual battle. Your children's hearts are being fought over and you play an integral role. Take the most shots. Be super intentional in speaking to and teaching your children about Jesus each and every day.

Offensive Strategy

One offensive strategy of soccer is to keep passing the ball (forward if possible) and to always keep moving. In this same way, we must not let our children's hearts or our methods of implementing the Gospel remain stagnant. Try new things. Be open to new opportunities for your children to listen and hear about Jesus.

Become a sponge when other moms offer advice. Do not be offended or intimidated when moms share strategies on how they disciple their children. Do not be afraid to ask either. Bring up the topic of discipleship in conversation. I am all ears when other moms and older women offer advice on how to biblically encourage my child. In the Bible, we are called to "listen to advice and accept discipline" (Prov. 19:20). This kind of openness to the ideas of others makes us wise. In the same way we want our children to listen and adhere to our advice, we must listen to the advice of others—women and other Christians who are also rooting for our child's success and spiritual growth.

It intrigues me that in Proverbs 19:20, the word "discipline" is interchanged for the word "instruction" in some Bible versions. Discipline is instruction. If we want to "take shots" at our children's hearts, we must also be diligent in disciplining our children. To discipline a child takes discipline. It is no easy task.

Disciplining is often laborious and seemingly unrewarding. But if we keep at it, if we are diligent to discipline and instruct our children all the days of their lives, then we can hope that someday, they will be counted among the wise. Through our wise counsel, the Lord is able to kindle their hearts. Do not give up. We can have hope that we will reap a bountiful harvest in watching our children's righteousness and godly character ripen and grow. Stay diligent. Spring is coming.

God wants to use us in some pretty big ways as mamas. The hearts of our children are impacted by our imparting of wisdom more than we know. Our children might roll their eyes or act like they do not care, but they hear every word that rolls off our lips. Instruct them passionately. Instruct them faithfully. Instruct them well.

Lord Jesus,
Give me words that are full of grace and salt today. Help me to take strides of faith in incorporating the Gospel message into my children's

hearts and daily lives. Show me ways to demonstrate Your love and help me be in sync with the Holy Spirit to know when the ball has been passed to me and I have an opportunity to take a shot. Help me to shoot with all my might.

In Jesus' heavenly Name, amen.

Steps of Faith:

- Be on the lookout for an opportunity to speak the name of Jesus, give God glory, or teach your children the meaning of grace in conversation when a teachable moment arises.

23
Discipline = Discipleship

"Whoever spares the rod hates their children, but the one who loves their children is careful to discipline them."

Proverbs 13:24

I HAVE HEARD IT SAID, "To spare the rod is to spoil the child." This saying is based on the Proverbs 13:24. This does not give you permission to beat your children or be abusive by any means. (If you are leaving a bruise, you are spanking too hard!) But it certainly does give you permission to be a nonpermissive parent who refuses to pacify their toddler's raging demands. I used to fall prey to this. My toddler would kick and scream and cry and whine to get what she wanted; and many times, I gave in. I felt weak and powerless. The more times that I gave in, the more powerless I became.

"The rod" referred to in Proverbs 13:24 is certainly an actual physical rod, but I believe there is a spiritual component to this verse as well. The rod is discipline. Discipline is twofold—the rod, in addition to Bible-based correction that is verbally stated (Prov. 29:15; Rev. 3:19). We are to discipline our children because we love them, and this is what God has called us to as parents.

Disciplining children is no fun and is often a draining task, but it is so rewarding in the long run. When I began disciplining my toddler for her temper tantrums and demands, I noticed a shift in her attitude. "I love you

Mommy," she would tell me way more often. I also got many more hugs. It is almost as if she was saying, "Thank you for correcting me."

It is not good for children to rebel, lie, demand, or be disrespectful. But it is even worse for them to get away with these things. It weighs heavily on their hearts. They need the rod of discipline delivered in tandem with reproof and godly wisdom. They need correction, and God's Word breathed into their little hearts and lives in the process. They need us to tell them right from wrong and point to Jesus in doing so.

Our children need us to discipline them. Their hearts are thirsty for our firm and loving correction. It makes them feel safe to know the boundaries and to have godly parameters surrounding them on all sides of their lives. It gives them a sense of security in knowing what is acceptable and godly and what is not. It gives them comfort in realizing that they cannot get away with committing willful sin in their lives. It empowers them to make right decisions based on their knowledge of the borders that exist.

Disciplining your children does not make them immune to sin. They will still act out and misbehave at times. They will still grapple with the serpent of sin in their lives, but we must prayerfully discipline and carefully correct our children when that sin rears its ugly head.

We do not have to be helicopter parents, but we do need to discipline our children when correction is called for. It is an outpouring of our love for the Lord. The Lord uses us as parents to discipline our children with discretion. Through godly discipline, we can be vessels of God's love and ultimate goodness in their lives.

The book of Hebrews tells us, "No discipline seems pleasant at the time, but painful. Later on, however, it produces a harvest of righteousness and peace for those who have been trained by it" (Heb. 12:11). Discipline is no fun to give or receive in the moment; but if our children can learn from their mistakes and have hearts that are aligned more closely to Jesus, they will thank us for it. They may never say thank you, but they might show you in other little ways. "I love you's," hugs, and attitude changes are forms of fruit that can be found that represent God's love growing up and out of our children's hearts.

Harsh discipline is terrible and detestable to the Lord (Eph. 6:4). Discipline without correction and God's Word incorporated is useless (Matt. 23:26). But discipline that is delivered with the heart of God in mind and God's Word on our tongues is pleasing to the Lord. Let us be faithful with the talents of our children's hearts the Lord has entrusted to us.

The Resurrection Power of Self-Control

When long days, temper tantrums, and ungrateful children threaten our sense of joy, let us cling to the cross and allow Christ's resurrection power to rise up in us. Before we blow a gasket, before we raise our voices, before we throw in the towel, let us draw from the well of Christ's living water that flows within us. No matter how deep that well seems, we must do the hard work to tug the rope through the pulley and elevate the bucket so that its purifying hydration can reach the depths of our parched souls. We could all use a cup of Christ's living water. The water Christ has to offer us lavishes our lives with grace, soothes our emotions, and quenches the torch of anger and disappointment that sometimes burns within us.

Children are not obedient toy soldiers. They have minds of their own. While this does not discount the fact that we should discipline our children when they choose rogue ways, it does attribute to the fact that we all fall short of God's glorious standard (Rom. 3:23). I think that how we handle our children's disobedience speaks volumes about God's love and grace. If we are able to react calmly with sound rationale, we teach our children to control their impulses, to bite their tongues, and to think twice before they act. This type of disciple requires the heart of God to be on the forefront of our minds all of the time.

We can acquire self-control through Christ's resurrection power within us, through the Holy Spirit. We have Jesus' power and authority pulsing through our veins. We must call upon Jesus' holy name and draw from the well of Christ's living water when we need a drop of patience to soothe our own shortcomings in regard to self-control. It is scientifically proven that children can process life lessons better when adults have their tempers under control. From a spiritual point of view, when we are calm in delivering discipline and correction, we are preaching the fruit of the Spirit, self-control.

We have access to the ultimate Source of peace and patience through Christ's resurrection. We have resurrection power in our lives flowing through our veins because of what Jesus did for us on the cross. Prayerfully harness that power. Dwell on having patience with your child and self-control in delivering consequences with biblical correction and God's heart in mind.

I have a confession: sometimes, I like to watch videos on social media that humorize certain sticky components of motherhood, such as:

- Toddlers adamantly following you to the bathroom, much like Samwise ruthlessly following Frodo on his quest in *Lord of the Rings.*
- Changing diapers of certain rambunctious toddlers being comparable to wrestling an alligator.
- Talking on the phone becoming nearly impossible because your little ones are making as much racket as an outdoor supermarket.
- Raising little girls being more like pandemonium mixed with rock-and-roll than soft singing and gently rocking baby dolls.

There are many hilarious videos I have seen that make light of some of the harder components of motherhood. Some actually bring tears to my eyes (because I am laughing so hard.) These videos strike a chord and lighten my soul. While they are making fun of the toddler-raising life, they enable me to step out of the moment and see the joy and light God had in mind.

While some moments of motherhood are so incredibly difficult, I cannot help but realize that these moments—which add up to days, which add up to years, which all too quickly equate to eighteen—are precious. So make the most of them! Make every moment count.

Some nights I pray, "Lord help me be a kind mom. Help me love my children well. And help me be firm, according to Your truth." I want to be a kind, sweet, and loving mom; but some moments of chaos leave me mystified, frazzled, and fuming. Anger is an emotion we must learn to harbor and keep at bay because we do not want yelling and fire in mom's eyes to be the legacy we leave. Furthermore, the more you yell, the more you will have to yell and continue to amplify your voice in order for your kids to respond.

Some moments of motherhood require us to be firm. But we can still be gentle. By ultimately having our hearts under control and not letting anger get the best of us, we can be godly examples of Christ's love. This is an area where I honestly struggle. I find myself slipping into patterns of raising my voice, only to repent and some weeks later start the pattern all over again. According to God's Word, we are to "not conform to the pattern of this world, but be transformed by the renewing of your mind" (Rom. 12:2). Only through Christ Jesus can this be made possible. When I remember my prayer, "Lord, help me be a kind mom. Help me to speak kindly and have grace in my tone of voice," it makes it a lot harder to trespass. Prayer is a much more powerful force than sheer will.

We need Jesus in our hearts, in our parenting lives. We need prayer spoken over us and our children each day. We need to focus on the fruits of the Spirit and weave "love, joy, peace, forbearance, kindness, goodness, faithfulness, gentleness, and self-control" (Gal. 5:22-23) into our everyday roles.

This does not come naturally. We have to be intentional. We have to be cognizant and have Jesus' presence ruling over us because we cannot do this on our own. I have heard it said, "Don't mom alone." But when we are alone and it is just us and our kids, Jesus is still watching. I want Him to be able to say, "'Well done, good and faithful servant!'" (Matt. 25:23).

Our children's hearts are like precious talents we have been entrusted to guard. Our example stretches farther than we know. Our kids will remember us and be impacted by our parenting for the rest of their lives (no pressure.) Fortunately, there is grace, and God's mercies are new each morning (Lam. 3:22-23). But most importantly, God is watching; and He calls us to be faithful mamas who bring Him glory and represent Jesus well.

> *Dear Jesus,*
>
> *I want to represent You well. Instill in me Your patience, which is drawn from a well much deeper than myself. Give me strength and endurance to pursue You, to do the heavy-lifting of pulling up the bucket of water with the rope and pulley You have provided through prayer, Your Word, and continual refocus on You. Give me patience for the sake of Your glory that I might reflect Your light in motherhood.*
>
> *In Jesus' life-giving Name, amen.*

Steps of Faith:

- Make a game plan in your mind or write it out if you need to. How will you respond the next time your son or daughter disobeys or sins against you or a sibling? You know your child's tendencies. It is better to have a preemptive plan before you are in the heat of the moment, trying to keep your cool and remember exactly how you wanted instances like these to play out. Think about it now.

- When it comes to discipline, you *do* want to help your children succeed and triumph over sin in their lives. You must intuitively prompt and direct them in developing patterns of peace, goodness, and right choices. Consider the analogy of potty-training a puppy dog. You do not want your puppy peeing on the carpet forever; therefore, when that puppy has an accident, you are quick to discipline it but then immediately take the dog outside to teach it the correct behavior. It is so important that we explain the heart of the matter when our children make mistakes and are quick to demonstrate the correct behavior and even make them practice it. No, our children are not puppies, but it is cruel to refuse a puppy or a child the right of learning from their mistakes, and instead keep them stuck. This could potentially frustrate a child and lead them to anger, which is what we are not supposed to do, according to God's Word (Eph. 6:4). We are called to raise our children in the discipline and instruction of the Lord. Godly discipline requires guidance from loving parents who desire to see their sons and daughters succeed and stomp out sin in their lives.

24
Hearts on Fire

"They asked each other, 'Were not our hearts burning within us while he talked with us on the road and opened the Scriptures to us?' . . . Then he opened their minds so they could understand the Scriptures."

Luke 24:32, 45

LUKE 24:32 AND 45 REFER to when Christ had been resurrected and was revealing Himself to chosen people. These were two disciples discussing the grave news of Jesus' death, but they did not even recognize Jesus initially. Only after Jesus broke bread with them later that evening were their eyes opened to the realization that this was the Messiah. Jesus has the ability to open the eyes of our hearts. He also has the ability to keep our eyes closed to certain spiritual or earthly matters. I believe Jesus does this as a means of protection.

The glorification factor was heightened after the two disciples realized it was Jesus all along. Sometimes, we are blinded to the reason as to why bad things happen. In God's timing, we will understand the purpose behind the pain, whether it is on this side of earth or in Heaven.

There are typically two reasons behind pain present in our lives. Ultimately, the purpose is to bring glory to God or to draw us near to His heart. In the case of Christ's crucifixion, the purpose checked both of these boxes. The purpose of Christ's death was to bring God glory in demonstrating

His resurrection power and to mend our relationship by reestablishing our eternal connection with Him.

loss

Losing a baby is the worst kind of pain. While I have not walked through this personally, in having children who are so dear to my heart, I can only imagine the degree of devastation. I am friends with several mothers who have walked through miscarriages. The pain seems disastrous, disorienting, disabling, and beyond difficult. Although the pain may never completely fade, Christ provides these mothers with a special portion of His Divine aid and care. The common unifying thread I have noticed in the lives of these mothers who know Jesus is that their faith is fortified after the fact. I have watched mothers struggle after losing a baby, but I have watched them rely on Christ and be overcomers in the name and by the power of Jesus.

After the rain, God placed a rainbow in the sky—a promise to never again flood the earth, a symbol of His love and ultimate goodness in our lives. While this rainbow may not always be the gift of another baby, God is the Source of our strength, our rainbow song after life's devastations. We all face tragedies and must intentionally seek God's rainbow after the storm, as David did when he wrote, "I lift up my eyes to the mountains—where does my help come from? My help comes from the LORD, the Maker of heaven and earth" (Ps. 121:1-2).

Through the pain and sorrow of life's losses, Jesus provides us hope and light. Even if it seems like you are engulfed in a sea of darkness, know that the sunrise is approaching, just beyond the horizon. God has good plans for you and me.

Be Prepared

My husband put an emergency ladder upstairs in my daughter Emma's closet. The ladder would be used in the case of a fire emergency, where the house was burning down and we were unable to get downstairs. While I do not foresee this type of event happening, I know that one day it very well could, and I am grateful for my husband's thoughtful preparation.

We all think that bad things will not happen to us; and when they do, we are shocked. Know that the seasons of life ebb and flow. You will experience hardship and trouble, but take heart and know that the Savior of the world holds you in the palm of His hand. Even when you are walking through the darkest of valleys, you are still in Jesus' cupped hands. He will carry you.

Realize and recognize the highs and lows of life and come to anticipate their patterns. While this will not eliminate the sting of the blow when trials strike, it will enable us to not be blindsided in the process. We can stand equipped and ready, fortified in faith, when we know that bad things are going to happen and we depend on the Lord to give us the strength and endurance to remain standing through it all. Let us live out Paul's words: "Be on your guard; stand firm in the faith; be courageous; be strong" (1 Cor. 16:13).

As mothers and Christ-followers, we are soldiers! We must take a stand for Jesus. The Gospel is our means of motivation. What Jesus did for us on the cross requires an obedient response. Through the thick-and-thin moments of motherhood and life, stay standing for the Lord. When you feel weak, call upon the name of Jesus; and He will give you the strength that you so desperately need.

Jesus is the Rock, our Firm Foundation. We must fortify our faith through God's Word and prayer. Spiritually prepare now for difficulties that lie ahead. Get in the Word and depend on it as your daily bread. Jesus is the Word. Build your house upon the Rock of Jesus and God's everlasting Word.

Jesus promised, "'I am the bread of life. Whoever comes to me will never go hungry, and whoever believes in me will never be thirsty'" (John 6:35). Come to Jesus through reading the Bible and connecting with the Lord through prayer. Experience life to the fullest in Christ. Jesus is the secret Ingredient for a life of contentment and peace. He gives us the ability to withstand any and all circumstances. The eternal joy that we have as believers through Christ carries us when the weight of the world is too much to bear.

God once said to Jeremiah, "'I have loved you with an everlasting love; I have drawn you with unfailing kindness'" (Jer. 31:3). "Everlasting" is a beautiful word. Its connotation is something we cannot wrap our minds around because the cord keeps unraveling, leaving a trail of Christ's mercy and faithfulness. I am thankful for the Lord's everlasting love. It is present in my life today and is guaranteed to be there all of my tomorrows.

Not everything in life is as lovely as the word "everlasting," but the good news is that these less-than-lovely things will fade away. Revelation 21:4 assures us, "'He will wipe every tear from their eyes. There will be no more death' or mourning or crying or pain, for the old order of things has passed away." The Lord will wipe away our every single tear. We can have hope and joy in today because our everlasting lives of tomorrow are secure in Christ Jesus.

Are You Ready?

One day, Jesus Christ will return. This is no secret among believers. We are to look forward to and long for this day with groaning in our hearts (Rom. 8:23). Eternity is written upon the heart of every human being, and those in Christ will experience eternity forever in Heaven with the Creator. Whether Christ will come back today or in a million years, we do not know. But we do need to be spiritually prepared for Christ's return.

Live out each day as if Jesus were coming back tomorrow. If we can consider our lives in this manner, taking one stride toward faithfulness and goodness after another, we will be encouraged and not feel like we are eating the entire elephant, all at once. We will stumble; we will make mistakes. But if we can take bite-sized approaches toward God's goodness and grace, we will cultivate sanctified hearts that are pleasing to the Lord. Live out each day with eternity in mind. Follow the words of Scripture: "Since then, you have been raised with Christ, set your hearts on things above, where Christ is, seated at the right hand of God. Set your minds on things above, not on earthly things" (Col. 3:1-2).

To be "raised with Christ" implies two things. One, we have been crucified with Christ, raised up from the ground, and have nailed our sin nature to the cross. Two, we have been resurrected with Christ, in that we have been called to a new life, one that is Spirit-filled and holy.

We have the gift of the Spirit of the living God abiding within us. Therefore, we must live life with hearts on fire for Jesus Christ. Live each day like it was your last. Cultivate a spirit that burns with passion for Jesus' approval and presence, a mind that craves God's Word like sustenance to starvation, and hands that approach life with eternal life in mind. Rekindle your heart to be set on fire for the Lord.

Second Peter 3:13 tells us, "But in keeping with his promise we are looking forward to a new heaven and a new earth, where righteousness dwells." God keeps His promises. Christ will return one beautiful day. We do not know the hour. Are you ready?

Dear Jesus,

Open the eyes of our hearts so that we can see the brevity of this life and focus on matters of eternity. Create in us pure hearts that long to know You more. Remake our minds to be molded according to Your goodness and truth.

Help us to rely on the Word for our daily bread. Jesus, we need more of You. Prepare us for what lies ahead in terms of death and new life found in You. Thank You for Your Holy Spirit, that we have the hope of eternal life someday.

In Jesus' heavenly Name, amen.

Steps of Faith:

- How can you spiritually prepare for Jesus' return? What small step can you take today and commit to that will enable you to know and grow in God's goodness?

- The next time you light a candle, gather around a campfire, or sit in front of a crackling fireplace, imagine Jesus' presence like He is there with you. Feel the warmth of His love. Acknowledge Him through a silent prayer.
- Jesus is love, grace, and goodness in full. He is hope, truth, and light. Thank Him for being these things for you today.

25
loving the least of These

"For we are God's handiwork, created in Christ Jesus to do good works,
which God prepared in advance for us to do."

Ephesians 2:10

AS A LITTLE GIRL, I remember watching my mom hand a lady a fifty-dollar bill in the mall parking lot. She had two crying babies in the car and needed gas money. Whether this lady was telling the truth or not, my mom did not care. She felt the Holy Spirit's tug on her heart. She listened and obeyed. I remember her example to this day. As believers and followers of Christ, we are called to do the same.

Sometimes, I feel like a failure when it comes to loving "the least of these." I get inwardly focused, and my vision for spotting those in need grows weaker and fades out. But through Christ, there is redemption. Through Christ, we can start anew. Through Christ, we can live out our days on the lookout for those in need.

The needs of these people span beyond the perimeter of ourselves. People need Jesus, plain and simple. They need His light. They need His warmth. They need His mercy and grace. They need His compassion. They need to know and experience the Lord's relentless love for themselves.

As Christians, we are living reflections of Christ. People should be able to feel Christ's warmth though us. They should experience Jesus' love through our generosity and willingness to walk the extra mile (Matt. 5:41-42).

When people's hearts are pierced by our love and kindness, it leaves a void for the Holy Spirit to enter through. When we take up our crosses and love the least of these, as Christ commands (Lk. 9:23), our hearts open up; and the Holy Spirit is able to pour into us and fill us in full so that we become living vessels, full of Christ's radiance and light, equipped and able to do "good works, which God prepared in advance for us to do" (Eph. 2:10).

Loving the Least of These From a Mama's Point of View

When Jesus describes how the righteous ones will be recognized at His return in Matthew 25, he says, "'The King will reply, "Truly I tell you, whatever you did for one of the least of these brothers and sisters of mine, you did for me"'" (Matt. 25:35-40). I believe that the words of these verses are quite literal. We are to feed the hungry, be hospitable, and give generously to those in need. We are to care for the sick, the elderly, and those in prison. I believe these things are 100 percent true. But I also believe that there are spiritual connotations to these Scriptures that apply to motherhood of which we should take note.

Our children are hungry for their daily bread. On a spiritual level, daily bread equates to the Word of God. We are to feed our children God's Word, because their souls are hungry for it. They need this nourishment for their minds and hearts to properly grow.

Our children are thirsty for the Living Water. Jesus is the Living Water. We be Jesus to our children by demonstrating God's love by turning the other cheek when insulted (Matt. 5:38-40), by choosing to not argue or complain (yes, not complaining is biblical! See Phil. 2:14), through forgiveness (Lk. 6:37), and by being on the lookout for those in need in our everyday lives. Lend someone the extra few dollars they request. Bring that family in crisis a meal. Love like Jesus and be on the lookout for ways you can bless others. Our children are thirsty. Let them see Jesus in you.

Jesus was a stranger when He was invited into the hearts and lives of His disciples. They left everything and immediately followed Him. Give other moms a chance. Even if you already have lots of friends and feel like your schedule has reached maximum capacity, reach out to other mamas and be a friend. You will never regret it.

Our children desire to be clothed in God's righteousness. We must adequately equip and prepare our children with the full armor of God, the wardrobe of the Fruits of the Spirit, and the attire of love. Scripture says, "Love is patient, love is kind" (1 Cor. 13:4). Are you demonstrating these simple truths in your own life?

Jeremiah 17:9 tells us, "The heart is deceitful above all things and beyond cure." At times, our children will fall prey to Satan's traps. When they do, we have a choice to make. Will we condemn them and leave them for the wolves, or will we humbly uplift them and share our own testimonies of God's unfailing grace? You have a choice to make. Choose to be the hands and feet of Jesus by sharing your own scars and resurrection story.

The resurrected King has resurrected us from sin and darkness. We are no better than "the least of these." We might be in a better situation or season of life, but we are all God's children, dearly loved. Because of Jesus' presence in our lives, we have been called and are equipped to be a light to our children and those in need. We are to bless others with the same measure of goodness and undeserved love that God has so generously gifted us.

You were created "for such a time as this" (Est. 4:14). Your example of working out God's truth in your own life is a testimony to your children. Your witness impacts their faith. You validate the name of Jesus and God's Word to your children when they see you living by the Word. Live well.

Lead your children to Jesus by being a light and source of strength to "the least of these." Grace the lives of your children and a hurting world in need of a Savior. His name is Jesus. Represent him for your children and all to see.

Serve people like you would serve Jesus. Bless others with the blessings He has so gracefully given you. Embrace the day with outstretched arms.

Cultivate a heart that is eager to do God's will through digging in the holy dirt of God's Word daily.

You are called and equipped for His Kingdom work, in your home and everywhere you go. Lead through acts of love, kindness, and generosity. Work diligently in serving others as if you were serving the Lord. Live out the command of Scripture: "Keep on loving one another as brothers and sisters. Do not forget to show hospitality to strangers, for by so doing some people have shown hospitality to angels without knowing it" (Heb. 13:1-2).

Live like Christ. Lead like Christ. Love like Christ. Let God's love set you free as you unleash it from your heart and allow it to cascade into your life.

> *Lord Jesus,*
>
> *Have Your way in my heart and life. Lead my hands and guide my feet toward loving others, especially "the least of these." I am no greater than the least of these because You looked down from Heaven and saw my desperate need.*
>
> *Thank You for sending Your Son, the ultimate act of love and sacrifice. Thank You for giving me eternal hope through the blood of Jesus. Show me ways to share Your everlasting joy with others in my everyday life.*
>
> *In Jesus' merciful Name, amen.*

Steps of Faith:

- Meditate on the following verses:
  - "'If anyone forces you to go one mile, go with them two miles. Give to the one who asks you, and do not turn away from the one who wants to borrow from you'" (Matt. 5:41-42).
  - "Then Jesus said to his disciples, 'Whoever wants to be my disciple must deny themselves and take up their cross daily and follow me'" (Matt. 16:24).

26
Cry Out to Jesus

"Let us then approach God's throne of grace with confidence, so that we may receive mercy and find grace to help us in our time of need."

Hebrews 4:16

I WAS SWITCHING OVER THE laundry when it happened. Fear lingering in the back of my mind, I quickly grabbed the wet, clean clothes and shoved them into the dryer. To leave two toddlers alone under any given circumstance is risky business. I did not hear a peep, not a sound; only a gut-wrenching instinctive mom feeling overtook me. I returned to the kitchen where I witnessed my almost two-year-old walking over to our brand-new bundle of joy with a mandarin orange in his hand.

"Josiah Jensen! We do not feed the baby!" I spouted.

I checked the inside of our newborn's mouth to make sure that he had not already given her a snack. To my shock and panic, I felt a lightning strike of fear surge throughout my entire body as I pulled out a raisin. Our newborn baby girl was one week old when this happened. Tears overtook me as I cried for what could have been and praised God for His shield of protection.

We cannot overcome the daily struggles of motherhood on our own accord. Mammoth-sized messes, constant business, laundry, cooking, cleaning, lunches to pack, diapers to change, errands to run, mile-long pick up lines to wait in—overcoming the daily struggles that motherhood entails takes a lot of prayer and pressing into Jesus. Only God is capable of covering us with His grace, infusing our hearts with His wisdom, and fortifying our lives with His peace and protection.

As moms, we need God. I dare say, we need God more than most; but the truth is, we all have a desperate need for Jesus. Some moments of motherhood cause me to cry out to Jesus loudly, while other moments are more peaceful as I rest in the palm of His hand. Either way, I know that God is always carrying me and holding me close.

Sometimes, my daughter Emma calls out to me while she is getting dressed. She is three years old and fully capable of putting her clothes on herself; but sometimes, something gets twisted or turned around, and she gets flustered and thinks she needs my help. So often, I do the same thing in my relationship with Jesus. When everything is going smoothly, according to plan, I feel self-sufficient, and my realization of Christ's presence fades into the background. When troublesome times and tumultuous trials strike, I cry out to Jesus.

Although we might feel like we need Him more at certain times than others, depending on our circumstances, He is near to us all of the time. Even when we do not see or feel His presence, God is still there. Scripture reminds us, "For the LORD will not reject his people; he will never forsake his inheritance" (Ps. 94:14).

The Power of Prayer

We need to pray. We need to pray fervently, adamantly, and consistently. Prayer is a discipline. The word "discipline" has a stern connotation, but I believe that prayer is something we can thoroughly enjoy. It is something we can come to love and long for. With Jesus present in our lives, the source of His great love, grace, and wisdom can flow in and out of us each day through prayer. Our connection with God can be like a breath of fresh air. We take in His love and exhale His grace unto others through our relationship with Jesus, God's Word, and prayer. Pray for God's grace. Ask for His forgiveness. Ask the

Lord to bring any hidden sin in your life to light so that you can know, love, and live for Jesus fully.

Pray with praise. Do not underestimate the power of thankfulness and a spirit of worship. God is pleased when you offer Him praise through prayer. Praise changes everything. It has the ability to empower and embolden our hearts and hands for Jesus. It adds salt to our otherwise-bland lives. Praise fortifies our hearts and lives with the illuminating power of Jesus Christ.

Pray for the Lord's protection. Ask God to keep your children and family healthy and safe. Sometimes, God gives us minor scares, like finding a raisin in your newborn's mouth, to warn you and ultimately keep you safe. We need to take note of and learn from the little lessons the Lord tries to teach us throughout the course of our lives. While I am not sure of the exact purpose behind the raisin scare, I can only assume it was a means of future protection. Ultimately, I thank God for His hand of safety surrounding my family.

Prayer is potent. Prayer is effective. Ask others who know and love Jesus to pray for you. The prayers of the righteous are powerful (Jas. 5:16). Our God is a God of specificity. He knows every detail of your life, down to the number of hairs on your head. Pray specific prayers. Similar to the way we delight in the details of our children's beautiful lives, the Lord delights in us, His beloved children.

Pray big. Nothing is too great for God, Who holds the universe in His hands. Nothing you ask for is deemed unworthy if it is positioned in your heart to serve the Lord and bring Him glory. The Lord sometimes plants grand ideas in our hearts that we should pray about and pursue. God-sized dreams are ultimately meant to bring God glory. Take confident steps toward the plans the Lord has for you. Take giant leaps when puddles are placed in front of you. The devil would like nothing more than to deem your plan or dream unworthy. He wants to cancel our plans to glorify God. When puddles come before you, take a leap of faith.

Do not be afraid to dive into the unknown waters of the Lord's grand design and purposes for you. Pursue the Lord in prayer, take a deep breath of

His grace, realize His favor, and jump on in. The Lord's loving arms will surely catch you. Our Heavenly Father wants little you standing on the edge of the pool to be brave. Jesus is calling your name. *Jump!* God has got you.

We can overcome the daily struggles in our lives through prayer. The Lord's grace covers and catches us when we fall. Through prayer, Jesus can pull us out of the pits into which we stumble. Lack of joy, discouragement, feelings of purposelessness, being overwhelmed, and moments of failure—God's grace can comfort and carry us through it all. Fingerprints of God's mercy and faithfulness can be found covering even our most desperate moments in motherhood.

Let your faith in Jesus allow you to float. Drop the anchor of prayer down deep into your heart and life. Let prayer keep you stationed nearby the lighthouse of Jesus' presence, power, and protection in your daily life.

> *Dear Jesus,*
>
> *I love You and long for Your presence in my life. Be with me. Guide, protect, and go before me. In motherhood and in life, lead me. Watch over my family and help me to keep a watchful eye on my children. Give me peace and balance in this endeavor. I love You and praise You for your goodness.*
>
> *In Jesus' perfect Name, amen.*

Steps of Faith:

- Jesus taught His followers to pray. His lesson was sweet and simple. Our prayers do not have to sound intricate or lovely. The Lord simply wants to hear from you. Try praying through Jesus' example prayer:

> *"This, then, is how you should pray: 'Our Father in heaven, hallowed be your name, your kingdom come, your will be done, on earth as it is in heaven. Give us today our daily bread. And forgive us our debts, as we also have forgiven our debtors. And lead us not into temptation, but deliver us from the evil one'" (Matt. 6:9-13).*

27
Grace-filled Mamas

"But grow in the grace and knowledge of our Lord and Savior Jesus Christ.
To him be glory both now and forever! Amen."

2 Peter 3:18

(THIS CHAPTER IS DEVOTED TO the voices of other Christian mamas sharing their grace-laced experiences, encounters with Jesus, and keynote lessons the Lord has taught them.)

Introduction

Motherhood was never meant to be easy; it is meant to make us holier. We can enjoy the little blessings along the way and praise Jesus through the storms because the Lord is good. Above our sticky circumstances, above our trials, above our errors, God is Sovereign. His plans are good.

In motherhood and life, God goes before us. Like the Israelites in the wilderness, God provides us with the shade of His presence during the day and the light and warmth of His goodness through our darkest nights. We can reach a better understanding of God's love for us in being a parent. We can adopt a heart and attitude of selfless giving through motherhood. We can sing a victory song over selfishness, control, loneliness, pride, impatience, and fear because of Jesus.

Being a mom is a sanctification process that is not always easy but one for which we can be so incredibly grateful. The following sections are a culmination of other women's stories about how Jesus has drawn them closer to God's heart through the refining, grace-filled process of motherhood.

Washing Machines and Grace
by Kathleen Knapp

As I stepped into the shower, I heard the loud screeching noise and smelled the acrid burning fumes. I knew right away the washing machine was stuck. I quickly grabbed my housecoat and rushed into the laundry room to stop the machine before the motor burned out. The room was filled with the pungent stench of an overworked motor. I opened the lid of the washing machine to find it full, very full—too full!

In an angry voice, I called my son to come and help me. Together, we pulled the cold, heavy, wet clothing and bedsheets from the washing machine onto the floor in a sloppy, soggy pile. As I looked in horror at how much he had pushed into the machine, I yelled at him angrily, reminding him of his laundry lessons, "This is too much, too heavy! And why are there so many jeans in here? Oh my goodness, you put your sheets in here, too! Haven't I told you?" On, and on, I spewed in my furious indignation.

I tried to be diplomatic, but I was failing miserably amidst my frustration as I stood with cold water swirling around my bare feet, sorting out the heavy, wet piles of cloth. We managed to separate the items into two piles and restart the washing machine with one load. The window was opened to let in the cold, fresh air. Ironically, the machine appeared no worse for wear after its ordeal. My son returned to his video game, and I returned to my shower.

While the rescued laundry continued lurching, I stood in the shower crying. You see, my son has autism; and sometimes, the "simple" life lessons take time and repetition to learn in his efforts for independence and autonomy. Sometimes, my patience and understanding are in short supply. Instead of being a "good mother," I chastised him out of anger. My tears reflected not just my frustration but also my guilt. "He's trying his best. I shouldn't have yelled."

As I took a deep breath, the tears subsided; and the still, small voice of the Holy Spirit spoke to me: "Have you never made mistakes? Have you never forged ahead on your own without listening or forgotten the instructions? Have you never failed? Yet by God's grace, you have been forgiven. Through Jesus' sacrifice, you have been shown grace and mercy."

Then I was reminded of the parable Jesus told about a man who was forgiven his large debt by the king. He was relieved but then demanded repayment of a small debt owed to him by a friend. The king heard of this and was outraged that the mercy shown to the man was not given in turn to his friend. He asked, "'Shouldn't you have had mercy on your fellow servant just as I had on you?'" (Matt. 18:33).

I was humbled and ashamed of my behavior and my hurtful words. I was convicted of lacking mercy and grace toward my son after the immense mercy and grace given to me by Jesus in forgiving my sins. I immediately prayed for forgiveness for my behavior.

After my shower, I got dressed and gently called my son. We hugged. I asked him to forgive me for yelling at him and for the hurtful things I said to him. I explained that sometimes, even parents make mistakes and need to ask for forgiveness. I reminded him of how much I love him and what a blessing he is to me and our family and how much God loves him, too. He apologized for the laundry mistake, and we cried together as we hugged again. As he helped me clean up the mess, we calmly talked about future strategies to plan the laundry size more efficiently and how to improve his independence skills for tasks.

I thank God for His grace in my life. I thank Jesus for forgiveness and mercy. I pray to be more graceful and understanding with my son and with others. I am so thankful for my son and all that he is learning as he grows into the strong and independent young man that God has planned for him to be. I am so thankful to be his mother. Together, we are learning. We are not perfect, but we are trying; and together, we'll make it—with mercy and grace, one load of laundry at a time!

Patience-A Refining Process
by Nichole Suvar

I always thought I was a fairly patient person. When other people would show frustration, I seemed to be able to keep my cool. When I worked as a therapist, coworkers would comment on how patient I seemed to be. In the realm of my Christian walk, I figured I at least had that virtue figured out. Then I met my daughter.

Hannah was born via C-section nine days early. We brought her home to her then eighteen-month-old brother. Having them so close together meant that I did not have to relearn the newborn stage because it felt like I had only just gone through it! I spent the first few weeks in the usual hazy, sleep-deprived state. Caring for a newborn while caring for a toddler kept me moving and exhausted. Yet I felt like I could get the hang of it with the help of my husband and mom (who, thankfully, lived close by!).

But at four weeks old, things changed. Hannah no longer nursed like she used to. In the previous weeks, she had gotten the hang of feedings and would eat in twenty minutes, ready for either a nap or a little interaction with her brother. But at a month old, she started to nurse for only a couple minutes and then would go into a hysterical screaming fit, followed by projectile spit-up. She was no longer interested in eating and instead would be inconsolable for close to an hour before she would finally fall asleep, exhausted.

Our days—and nights—progressed to this: three minutes of feeding, screaming, spit-up, screaming, sleep, repeat. The only way I could keep her content was upright in a baby carrier strapped to my chest. We did laundry, dishes, vacuuming, and everything else together.

A doctor appointment revealed the answer: acid reflux. Because of her young age, we were told she would grow out of it. Medication was not advised, but a few over-the-counter remedies were offered. We tried everything. Nothing soothed her. So we continued our routine of a couple minutes of feeding, screaming, spit-up, screaming, sleep, repeat—and prayed she would grow out of it quickly.

She eventually did—but it took nine months. Nine months, out of a lifetime, does not seem like much. But when you are in the middle of it and have no idea when it will end, it seems like an eternity.

My children are teenagers now, and I have no doubt I still have some missteps of parenting ahead of me. However, in my seventeen years of parenting so far, those nine months are my most regretful. The constant crying and my lack of being able to console stretched every threadbare bit of patience I ever had.

Looking back over that time, I am reminded of 2 Corinthians 12:9: "'My grace is sufficient for you, for my power is made perfect in weakness.' Therefore I will boast all the more gladly about my weaknesses, so that Christ's power may rest on me." I had thought I was a patient person. But in reality, I just had not come across a situation in my young adult life to truly test how little patience I possessed. I had taken pride in my own "achievement" when, in reality, I was weak. There were many times that I felt like I was at a breaking point and I had to lay Hannah down, screaming, in her crib and walk away, afraid of what I would do in my frustration. It is to my shame that I write these words. I wish I could go back to those nine months and do it differently. I would love to hold that screaming Hannah and speak soothing words of love and swaddle her in my arms while swaying to the rhythm of a lullaby. I would love another chance to show patience in the midst of her pain that she could only communicate by piercing screams.

Of course, these deep regrets in parenting do not allow us to have do-overs. However, they do allow us to learn and apply. Now I know that any patience I possess is not of my own merit. Now I know that I can claim my weakness and look to Jesus to make me strong. Now I know that I have the power of Christ in me when I can give up my own weak, human strength and firmly stand in the power of His Holy Spirit in my life.

Though I was given the testing of patience during that time, I was also given much grace by God as I walked through the fire as a young mom. Our children are part of our refining. We look to teach them about life; but in reality, they teach us what life is all about.

I share this to encourage the mom who feels she is drowning in her own shame and regret over how she handled a past parenting mishap. God extends grace. Take your claims of weakness and feelings of shame to Him and ask for forgiveness, strength, and wisdom to move ahead. Like my proud outlook on my own patience, my daughter came along to show me I was not nearly as patient as I made myself out to be. I could have patience only so far in my own strength; the only fruit of true patience could be brought about by the power of His Spirit.

And when I took the sin of my own pride and admitted I needed Jesus to help me love my daughter as I should, then He could work through my heart and start refining me to become more like Him and less like me.

Surrender
by Lindsay Morris

Motherhood is a journey. On each leg of your journey, you will venture through various trials that have the potential to develop character in you. These trials will either make or break you. The part of the journey of motherhood I am currently on is *surrender*.

Surrender—because I cannot force my three-year-old son Jude to potty-train. I have read the books. I have used all sorts of bribing techniques and "pick your own undies" motivations. But you cannot force another human to go to the bathroom. So I surrender. I am not giving up. I am not throwing in the towel and saying, "Forget it. I guess my kid will just go to college in diapers!" I am giving it to God and asking that He work on little Jude's heart to have the desire to potty-train.

Surrender—I learned that lesson the hard way a couple of years ago when my son Luke was in the longest season of swim lessons with no progress that any human being has perhaps ever endured. Luke attended swim lessons for two years every Thursday at 4:35 p.m. from the ages of three to five. Miraculously, every time when we left the pool, his hair was still dry because the kid refused to put his head underwater. Essentially, swim lessons were happening, but he was not really learning to swim.

I am not the type of mom who was trying to get her kid to become a future Michael Phelps. I just wanted him to learn to swim as a practical life skill. There were so many times during those two years of swim lessons when I thought, "Forget it. This kid is so stubborn. We are just going to quit swim lessons for now." But God nudged my heart to surrender. Surrendering is not the same as giving up. Giving up is quitting. We can surrender our will but still very much be in the game. When we surrender our will, God has room to move.

Typically, Luke had very sweet, docile female swim instructors in their teens or twenties. But one day, Mr. Hoss (a nickname that was quite appropriate for his hulking six-foot-seven frame) was his substitute swim instructor. I am not sure exactly what was said, but Mr. Hoss gave Luke a good, old-fashioned, male role model pep talk; and by the end of the lesson, Luke was swimming unassisted for the first time. He was even putting his head underwater! Since that day, his swimming skills have improved; and he now loves swimming.

Being a mother will give you so many opportunities to surrender. Every challenge can be met with the choice for you to have three basic responses:

1. Give up.
2. Keep going, but worry and fret.
3. Surrender.

Most women are extremely resilient and will not just give up when met with challenges in their lives and in the lives of their children. But how will you approach challenges? Matthew 6 talks about how we cannot add a single day to our lives by worrying. If God feeds the birds, how much more will He take care of you?

We can trust that God has the best interests of our children in mind. Some things just take time. Things like potty-training, learning to ride a bike, learning to tie shoelaces, etc. And then, there will be other times, maybe when our kids are adults, when we have to trust God in a whole new way—when our child has strayed from God, when they are dating someone who is not a Christ-follower, when they are battling addiction.

I like how Dale Wilsher defines surrender in the book *What's Your Mom Type?* "Surrender is laying down your own agenda. Surrender is relinquishing what you consider your own. Surrender allows God to be the authority, not only in your life, but in the lives of your children."[7]

While surrender may feel helpless and even hopeless, neither of those is true. Surrender is the means to true victory because the moment you surrender your desires, your concerns, and even your children to God, He is in control. They are now in His hands, and He will be victorious.

Will you surrender your concerns about your children to the Lord? What worries are you battling concerning your children that you need to hand over to Him? Let us follow Jesus' instruction:

> "Therefore I tell you, do not worry about your life, what you will eat or drink; or about your body, what you will wear. Is not life more than food, and the body more than clothes? Look at the birds of the air; they do not sow or reap or store away in barns, and yet your heavenly Father feeds them. Are you not much more valuable than they? Can any one of you by worrying add a single hour to your life?" (Matt. 6:25-27).

---

7   Dale Wilsher, *What's Your Mom Type?: Discovering God's Design for You* (Morgan Reid Press, 2019), 73.

Let Go and Let God
by Brianna Barrett

I found my way back to Jesus through my son's birth. My son was born with small holes in his lungs due to premature birth. He ended up with bilateral chest tubes and a ventilator on his first day alive. Those nights between my hospital discharge and being able to bring him home were some of the most tortuous ones I have ever endured. A mother should never have to experience leaving the hospital without her baby in tow.

When I got home, I did not know what to do. I did not want to be there; I wanted to be at the hospital. It did not matter that the medical staff had all but ordered me to go home because I "needed my rest." Clearly, they had never been sent home without their baby because there was no resting. I did not want to sit around and watch TV or read; never mind the fact that I could not focus on anything enough to concentrate. I could not clean because there was nothing else to clean (hello, nesting!).

Despite the complications through Jackson's birth and first days, my milk did come in; and I was on a rigorous schedule for pumping. He took in a lot of calories, due to his size at birth; and the nurses encouraged me to pump every three hours. They wanted me to keep up production, hoping that one day I would be able to naturally feed him. On that first night at home, I was up pumping; so I called the hospital to check on Jackson. They assured me nothing had changed from when I had last called at ten.

As I sat in my new glider rocker holding those milk bottles, I burst into tears, crying out to God, "God, I know that I haven't talked to You in a while. But I will do whatever You want if You will just save my baby." This prayer changed my life. I continued, between sobs, to plead and bargain with God for a few more minutes, hoping that He would heal and save my son.

That prayer began to change my midnight feedings. At the next feeding time, I dug out the Bible in my nightstand drawer and started reading. I kept up with my prayer. "God, please heal Jackson. Please don't let him die; please save him."

Over the course of the next few days, I spent my time pumping in prayer and Bible reading and during the times that I sat at the hospital with him in vigil. I asked everyone I knew to pray for him; it could not hurt.

Little by little, Jackson was making progress, but my prayers did not stop. He was first weaned off the ventilator, and then the tubes were removed. As the healing progressed, I continued to use my pumping times to pray for Jackson. Gradually, I started praying about other things, including my marriage. The late nights became my time with God. I was honest and raw, and there was no fluff or show in my prayers.

When Jackson came home, we rejoiced; but I remember that first night. I was scared and did not really know exactly what to do. It had been a couple of weeks since he was born, and I was afraid that he would stop breathing again. So my next prayer started, "God, I have no clue what I am doing; help me. Keep my baby safe and healthy." That became my prayer. I would feed Jackson, and then I would pump. While Jackson was awake, I would read the Bible; and when I got anxious about something, I would sing hymns that I remembered singing as a child. Those songs brought me peace.

When he had fallen asleep and was back in his crib, I began the pumping and praying cycle all over again. I fell asleep with that pump on more times than not. Over time, it became easier to talk with God. I continued reading the Bible and memorizing Scripture. The late-night Bible study eventually became an early-morning study before anyone else in the house gets up. The prayers for my son have not ceased; as I clean or drive, I keep on talking to God.

One day, my husband said, "You talk to Jesus like you are sitting across from a friend having coffee." In my relationship with Jesus, He is a Friend. I call on Him constantly to share my innermost thoughts and often refer to Him as "Papa." Over time, as I dug deeper into the Word, He responded with verses; and sometimes, when I am still, I hear Him answer. Through my experiences in motherhood, my relationship with Jesus has grown from a lukewarm acquaintance to a woman after God's own heart who cannot seem to get enough of the Word. Over the last decade and a half, my relationship with Jesus has continued to grow, as has my son's relationship with his Heavenly Father.

A time that I would define as one of the worst in my life showed me how God works things out for His good (Rom. 8:28). I could not see it at the time, but my uncertain situation caused me to depend on and trust in God. Other moments in this journey into motherhood had me crying out to God late in the night—not knowing how things would turn out and having to blindly trust that God was in control and that things would work out for His good. I am a woman who likes to be in control, but God has softened that need. I have a little mantra that has helped: "Let go, and let God." God is in control. We have to let go and release our children, our marriages, ourselves, and everything else to God. My husband often gently reminds me of this.

Dear Heavenly Papa,

Thank You for blessing me with motherhood and my children. Lord, they are truly a gift from You. Thank You for not giving up on me, and for bringing me back to You. Lord, sometimes I do not see how something is going to work out, but You know; nothing is a surprise to You. That brings me comfort and peace, knowing You have got this under control. Forgive me for my doubt and desire to be in control. I trust You, Lord; and when I falter, would You help bring my heart and mind back into alignment with Yours? Thank You.

In Jesus' Name, Amen.

Steps of Faith:

- What is God telling you that you need to turn over to Him? Let go and let God.
- When mountains in motherhood arise, use the following Scriptures to help you climb:

- "'Come to me, all you who are weary and burdened, and I will give you rest'" (Matt. 11:28).
- "If I make my bed in the depths, you are there" (Ps. 139:8).
- "Even the darkness will not be dark to you; the night will shine like the day, for darkness is as light to you" (Ps. 139:12).
- "He said to her, 'Daughter, your faith has healed you. Go in peace and be freed from your suffering'" (Mark 5:34).

28
Sanctified Motherhood

*"May God himself, the God of peace, sanctify you through and through. May
your whole spirit, soul and body be kept blameless at the coming of our Lord
Jesus Christ. The one who calls you is faithful, and he will do it."*

1 Thessalonians 5:23-24

SANCTIFICATION IS THE WORK OF Jesus Christ. The blueprints for a
sanctified life can be found through God's Word. Sanctification is not of or
from ourselves. Sanctification has the fingerprints of the Holy Spirit written
all over it. Through prayer, God's Word, and steadfast obedience, we are called
and equipped to follow His lead.

Whether you are on a mountain high or valley low point in motherhood,
your faith walk, or life, the Lord can deliver you and give you the strength
to stand. Even when we walk through the darkest of valleys, we are still in
the embrace of Jesus' folded hands. Not only can the Lord pull you through,
but He can also equip you to run this race in such a way that will qualify
you not only as a finisher but also as one who gets a prize. You are Christ's
prized possession, dearly loved, and made holy through His blood. For no
other reason than Christ Himself, you are called and equipped to lead.

In motherhood and in life, run to receive the prize. Honor Jesus with
your whole heart, your time, talent, and treasure (Matt. 6:19-24). Adopt the
disciplines of a godly woman and walk growing "in wisdom and stature, and

in favor with God and man" (Lk. 2:52). Use whatever gifts the Lord has given you to faithfully serve the Lord. Take a leadership role in the stewardship of God's grace by giving back to others what God has so gracefully given you (1 Pet. 4:10). Jesus adores you. Live from the source of His great love.

"Love the Lord your God with all your heart and with all your soul and with all your mind and with all your strength." These red-letter words, found in the Bible in Mark 12:30, were spoken by Jesus, sanctified, and made holy by His blood. There are components of this verse that are often overlooked or downplayed that should be highlighted and celebrated as moms and Christ-followers. The four components of loving God, as Jesus' first and greatest commandment, are loving God with your heart, soul, mind, and strength. The first two come more naturally to me than the latter. As a mom, it is easy to love God because of His holy nature; but loving God with my life through my thoughts and with my free time and surrendering control in all areas become more of a challenge.

Jesus began His ministry on earth around age thirty, the same age David was when he began his reign as king of Israel. I love noticing the parallels or foreshadows of Christ that can be found in the Old Testament when we look closely in studying God's Word. King David was not a perfect example, but as "a man after [God's] own heart" (1 Sam. 13:14), there is much wisdom we can glean from the life of David. David was not tall or kingly in terms of physical appearance; but he loved the Lord God with his whole heart, soul, mind, and strength. David spent his hours writing psalms, or praises, to God in the fields when he was a shepherd before his kingship. He lived a life of worship and used his free time to glorify God. Even when he stumbled, he was quick to repent, lament, seek redemption, ask for forgiveness, and accept God's grace.

Jesus was the quintessential example of a person who loved the Lord God with all His heart, soul, mind, and strength. He loved God with His whole heart for His entire life. Jesus lived for the Lord and made physical sacrifices in order to follow God and live out the Holy Spirit's promptings in His life.

He made the greatest sacrifice of all in His death on the cross but fully trusted in God's plan and, on the third day, rose again.

I am totally and completely in love with Jesus. But that does not mean that I do not experience trials and temptations in motherhood and in life. The Lord has to help me choose self-control, to come alongside my children with humility and grace in my heart, even when they sin against me, each other, and the Lord God. I cannot control their hearts. I must discipline my children out of love; but first and foremost, I must teach them of our desperate need for Jesus because we "all have sinned and fall short of the glory of God" (Rom. 3:23).

I am no different than my children in terms of having sin. I am no different than my children in terms of the magnitude of God's love for me. The difference between me and my children is my leadership role in their lives. I have been given this miraculous, grand assignment to impart my children with the knowledge, love, and wisdom of God's Word that can only come alive in their hearts through the power of the Holy Spirit.

There is no formula to motherhood. The key is Christ in me—depending on His strength and power over my own and putting on the heart, soul, mind, and strength of Jesus each day. In this way, I can be the best mother that I can be.

Christ is working in me, purifying my heart and ridding me of the mud and muck as I mother my children and learn what it is to be childlike, pure in heart, and humble. Leaning in on Christ and letting the King become my all is a purification process that I am willing to weather because "I know that my Redeemer lives" (Job 19:25). Jesus is alive in me and wants me to take up my cross each day. He is grooming my heart, soul, mind, and strength to reflect God's own heart.

All of this is made possible through the power and presence of the Holy Spirit. Apart from Christ, I am incapable of cultivating the attributes of a mother whose heart beats solely and completely for the Lord God. The first and greatest commandment of fully loving the Lord with every fiber of our being is impossible without the presence of Jesus in our daily lives. So I encourage you to get into the Word, follow the Holy Spirit's promptings in your life, give thanks, develop a lifestyle of worship, and let Jesus take the wheel of your heart.

The intersection of motherhood and faith is a cruciform story. It calls us out and commands us to obey. It reshapes our hearts and lives to be conformed into the pattern of Christ's likeness. It is laced with God's grace and miraculous strength that covers our weaknesses. First Corinthians 6:11 says, "And that is what some of you were. But you were washed, you were sanctified, you were justified in the name of the Lord Jesus Christ and by the Spirit of our God." What Paul is referring to in this beautiful illustration is that our former carnal state of mind and lifestyle has been washed away and sanctified through Christ Jesus. When we mother with Christ as our backbone, "His grace is sufficient: (2 Cor. 12:9). The cross cancels out our sins and former mom failures. We can mother in the light of redemption because of Jesus. Romans 8:6 encourages us, "The mind governed by the flesh is death, but the mind governed by the Spirit is life and peace."

Before becoming a mom, I was selfish in need of a Savior. I considered myself first before others and sometimes even before God without consulting the Lord in prayer. I would say and do what I considered was best for number one—me. At the time, there was no laughter and make-believe play in the background. There was no kissing boo-boos, pushing swings, or passing out popsicles. It was just me, my husband, and our dog, Molly. Logistically speaking, life was simpler back then. But life was not as full. It was not as full of joy. It was not as full of fun. It was not as full of selfless giving and small sacrifices. Without children in the picture, life was of a lesser caliber. Children brought abundance, joy, and God-given purpose into my life.

There is a reason that the Bible commands us to "be fruitful and multiply" so many times (Gen. 1:28, 9:1, 9:7, 28:3, 35:11). The psalmist adds, "Children are a heritage from the Lord, offspring a reward from Him" (Ps. 127:3). These words are true. While not all moments in motherhood are picture perfect, all of the components culminate into something that is timeless, lovely, and true. Motherhood illustrates a picture of something that is God-inspired and uniquely beautiful.

There is a reason why Solomon wrote the lyrics of Psalm 127:3. The Lord planted these words in Solomon's heart and mind. God gave him a pen as a tool of worship and said, "Write for me." What has God called you to do for His glory? Make disciples in your home and everywhere you go. Do not hide the light God has given you. Let it shine.

Solomon was a parent himself. He was also a child of God. We are blessings to the Lord as His children and image-bearers. We love our children in a similar way that God loves us. We can understand the Lord's love for us more fully in having children of our own.

Glorify God through parenthood. Let each day bear witness to the fact that "you are a chosen people, a royal priesthood" (1 Pt. 2:9) as a mom and wife. You have been called and created for such a time as this. By the power of Christ, mother with all your might and let Jesus do His sacred, holy work in sanctifying the conditions of your heart. Allow Jesus to break up the hard grounds inside of you. Let Christ in to plow and plant seeds deep within the secret depths of your spirit through motherhood. Allow your faith in Jesus to intersect with your daily life as a mom and form the cross of Christ for your children and the world to see.

Dear Jesus,

Thank You for Your great love. Thank You for the gift of Your precious blood. Please make me holy and make me new. I want my whole life; heart, soul, mind, and strength to honor You. Help me to live from the source of Your great love. Equip me and show me how to lavish Your love and grace upon others. Create in me a pure heart whose motives are to please You.

Help me to be a strong mom, equipped with the sword of Your Word. Give me wisdom to abide in Your strength and might (Eph. 6:10). Help me to bless my children and the world all around me. As a daughter of Eve, show me creative ways to nurture the world and those within my sphere of influence.

Paint my world with Your bright colors; and when I muddle and mess up the paint mixing red, blue, and yellow to create a muddy shade of brown because of my sin, Jesus, forgive me. You are "the pioneer and perfecter of [my] faith" (Heb. 12:2). I want your initials evident, spelled out on every page of my life. I want the red letters of Your spoken Word to come alive in me.

Lord, do a holy work in my heart and life. Consecrate me. Come alongside me as I endeavor to fulfill the purification process of knowing and growing closer to your heart. Rid the deep waters of my soul of any impurities so that I can wholly and fully reflect Your goodness and glimmering light. Sanctify me as a mother, wife, and daughter of Christ.

In Jesus' sacred Name, amen.

Steps of Faith:

- State the following benediction. Speak these words over your life and let them soak down deep into your heart: "I can do anything, and all things that God leads me to. The Lord has placed my babies in my arms for a specific, special, sacred reason. Through motherhood, God is going to guide me. Through motherhood, God is going to uplift me. Through motherhood, God is going to hold me close. As I lead and feed my children, the Lord is leading and feeding me. With every sacrifice made, load of laundry accomplished, lunch packed, diaper changed, and bedtime prayer, the Lord is sanctifying my heart. Thank You, Jesus, for the gift of my children. Thank You for making me in Your image and blessing me with these small blessings to call my own until they are fully grown. Thank You for the gift of motherhood. May it refine me and draw me closer to Your heart. In Jesus' holy, mighty, wonderful, faithful, merciful, magnificent, precious, perfect, righteous, redeeming, fully sanctified, grace-filled name, amen!"

AFTERWORD
Simple Truths

"Whatever you do, work at it with all your heart, as working for the Lord, not for human masters, since you know that you will receive an inheritance from the Lord as a reward. It is the Lord Christ you are serving."

Colossians 3:23-24

SOMETIMES, I FEEL LIKE MY world around me is spinning. I get overwhelmed in motherhood and in life. My toddler's business does not stop. My four-year old's questions are an endless waterfall. My nine-month old's need to be fed and looked after with acute care does not end. The dishes continue to need cleaning; the laundry keeps on coming; and hungry bellies require my cooking. No, the world does not stop spinning; but through Christ, we can have hope and joy throughout our days.

When the tempest sweeps in and the demands of life batter you without end, remind your heart of these simple truths:

- I am unique (Ps. 139).
- I am loved (John 3:16).
- I am chosen (1 Pt. 2:9).
- I am washed, sanctified, and justified (1 Cor. 6:11).
- I am covered in God's grace (Eph. 2:8).
- I am carried by Christ's strength (2 Cor. 12:9).

Let the current of Christ's love and grace carry you downstream, out of the storm. Remember, you are doing a good job, Mama. Motherhood is not always easy; but if we approach it as if we are working for the Lord, it will be rewarding. Jesus loves you. Always remember this truth.

I will close with these words from Colossians:

> My goal is that they may be encouraged in heart and united in love, so that they may have the full riches of complete understanding, in order that they may know the mystery of God, namely, Christ, in whom are hidden all the treasures of wisdom and knowledge . . . So then, just as you received Christ Jesus as Lord, continue to live your lives in him, rooted and built up in him, strengthened in the faith as you were taught, and overflowing with thankfulness (Col. 2:2-3, 6-7).

This is my prayer for you! Be encouraged by the Word. Live uplifted by His love. Acquire godly wisdom through Christ by reading the Bible. Live your life rooted in Christ Jesus, built up and strengthened by the power of God's Word and prayer. Let your heart be glad. May your spirit overflow with thanksgiving because Jesus is alive and doing a mountain-moving, nation-building, tribe-transforming work in you as a mother and daughter of the Lord Most High.

Live set free. Live sanctified.

Bibliography

"5 C's of Diamonds (Yes, 5): How to Select The Perfect Engagement Ring, The." The Natural Diamond Council. July 2, 2020. www.naturaldiamonds.com/engagement-and-weddings/how-to-select-the-perfect-engagement-ring.

MacFadyen, Heather. "Signpost Parenting: Ann Voskamp [ep. 394]." January 30, 2023 in *Don't Mom Alone*. Podcast audio. 55:07. https://heather-macfadyen.com/2023/01/30/signpost-parenting-ann-voskamp-ep-395.

Mickelson, Jonathan K. "Christianos (a Christian) Χριστιανός, וְחֹזִ֫ישְׁמ, Unabridged Version." Greek4Christians, 2021. greek4christians.com/@Vocabulary_Topics/Special_Vocabulary~Christianos%2C_Unabridged_version.

Rider, Elizabeth. "7 Types Of Love (And What They Mean)." Elizabeth Rider, Inc. Accessed October 13, 2023. www.elizabethrider.com/7-types-of-love-and-what-they-mean.

TerKeurst, Lysa. *The Best Yes.* Nashville: Thomas Nelson, 2014.

Wilsher, Dale. *What's Your Mom Type?: Discovering God's Design for You.* Morgan Reid Press, 2019.

About the Author

ALEXANDRA "ALEX" JENSEN IS A steering team leader for the Mothers of Preschoolers organization, commonly known as "MOPS." She has two published books: *A Beautiful Season: Finding Your Identity in Christ After a Dating Relationship Ends* and *The Meaning of Motherhood: Discovering Joy and Purpose through Christ in the Everyday Moments of Mom Life*. Alex and her husband attend Battlecreek Church in Tulsa, Oklahoma. Alex has a bachelor's degree in elementary education with a creative writing minor and a master's degree in math and science education. She is a former elementary school teacher. Alex is a wife, stay-at-home mother of three, and antiques dealer.

For more information about
ALEXANDRA JENSEN
please visit:

www.alexandrajensen.org

Coming Soon from Alexandra Jensen

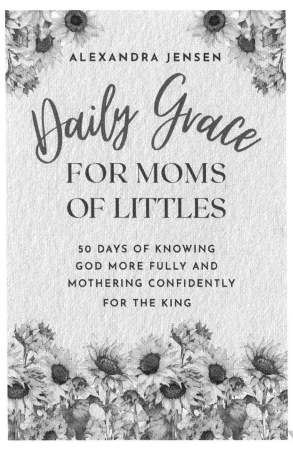

ALEXANDRA JENSEN

Daily Grace

FOR MOMS OF LITTLES

50 DAYS OF KNOWING
GOD MORE FULLY AND
MOTHERING CONFIDENTLY
FOR THE KING

Ambassador International's mission is to magnify the Lord Jesus Christ
and promote His Gospel through the written word.

We believe through the publication of Christian literature, Jesus Christ and
His Word will be exalted, believers will be strengthened in their walk with
Him, and the lost will be directed to Jesus Christ as the only way of salvation.

For more information about
AMBASSADOR INTERNATIONAL
please visit:

www.ambassador-international.com

Thank you for reading this book!

*You make it possible for us to fulfill our mission, and we are grateful for
your partnership.*

*To help further our mission, please consider leaving us a review on your social
media, favorite retailer's website, Goodreads or Bookbub, or our website.*

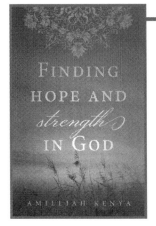

Finding Hope and Strength in God is a twelve-month devotional with different themes for each month focused on pointing you to your all-sufficient Savior, Who will give you strength and hope to face the day and to live a meaningful and fulfilling Christian life. Its practical approach to life will help you navigate real-life situations with tangible solutions to help you find meaning, hope, strength, and courage despite the tumultuous eventualities of life.

When Kathy Vintson finds herself upside down with her underwear on full display at, she suddenly realizes just how chaotic the world can be, and she is reminded of the Crown Effect—that she is a daughter of the King, Whose unmerited favor is to love her, even when her granny panties are on full display. Using humor and humility as her guide, Kathy takes a deeper look into what it means to be truly loved by the King of kings and how to bask in His love and peace, even when the world feels like it is closing in.

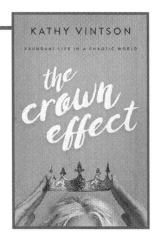

In *#NoFilter: Unmasking the Woman God Created You to Be*, Jodi Hendricks helps you challenge the filters that have enslaved you, discover the calling to which you've been called, and to bask in the truth that as creatures of the Creator Himself, you need no filter. The Almighty Who created you has had a plan and a purpose for you since you were knit together in your mother's womb, and He has called you to walk in a manner worthy of this calling.

Made in the USA
Columbia, SC
22 March 2025

55499606R00100